P9-CLC-419

Praise from many directions for

Soul to Soul

"*Soul to Soul* is a sensitive, courageous, and
compelling journey to wisdom."
—Brian L. Weiss, author, *Many Lives, Many Masters*

"*Soul to Soul* is beautiful, self-affirming, *and* globally healing.
It delves into the worlds of compassion and connectivity
and soothes the soul with timeless wisdom."
—Mike Myers, comedian and actor

"*Soul to Soul* is a reminder to me of who we are
and what it means to be a human being."
—Kenny Loggins, singer and songwriter

"An astonishingly clear, accessible guide to living an authentic,
truly empowered life. *Soul to Soul* is a wonderful read
that combines practicality with genuine wisdom."
—Marc Goldstein, M.D., Surgeon-in-Chief, Male Reproductive
Medicine, New York Presbyterian Hospital, Cornell Medical Center

"This book will take you beyond the boundaries of your own
conditioning to true spiritual freedom."
—Deepak Chopra, author of *Buddha: A Story of Enlightenment*

"This is one of those books that make you feel the author had
you specifically in mind when he wrote it, because he speaks
directly to the very issues you are struggling with in your life.

It is simple, clear, wise and profound. A must-read for everyone dedicated to the growth of soul in their lives."

—Ellen Burstyn, Academy Award–winning actress
and author of *Lessons in Becoming Myself*

"*Soul to Soul* is full of wisdom from someone who lives 'a deeply felt life,' and presents it with eloquence and transparency. You will want to read and reread it, savoring every page of its transformative power."

—T. Byram Karasu, M.D., Chairman of the Department of Psychiatry,
Albert Einstein College of Medicine

"*Soul to Soul* has the potential to transform your experience. You will find yourself returning to it again and again."

—Colin Slade, Senior Vice President and
Chief Financial Officer, Tektronix, Inc.

"A heartfelt book of wisdom about life and our empowering capacity to change."

—Alexander Astin, Professor Emeritus of Higher Education, UCLA

"*Soul to Soul* is wonderfully clear and insightful. It provides so many meaningful answers to some of the most fundamental questions anyone could ask."

—Herb Alpert, legendary jazz musician and sculptor

*f*P

ALSO BY GARY ZUKAV

The Dancing Wu Li Masters:
An Overview of the New Physics

The Seat of the Soul

Thoughts from the Seat of the Soul:
Meditations for Souls in Process

Soul Stories

WITH LINDA FRANCIS

The Heart of the Soul:
Emotional Awareness

Thoughts from the Heart of the Soul:
Meditations on Emotional Awareness

The Mind of the Soul: Responsible Choice

Self-Empowerment Journal:
A Companion to the Mind of the Soul

Guide to Gary Zukav's Books

Each book is a stand-alone experience.
They are all perfect starting points, so use your intuition.

Soul to Soul:
**Communications
from the Heart** (2007)

Thoughts from
The Seat of the Soul:
**Meditations for Souls
in Process** (1994)

Soul Stories
(2000)
Illustrates some ideas in
The Seat of the Soul,
and more, with stories

The Seat
of the Soul
(1989)
The key book—about soul,
evolution, and authentic
power

The Heart of the Soul:
Emotional Awareness (2001)
(with Linda Francis)
*In-depth explanation, experiential
learning, and practical applications*

The Mind of the Soul:
Responsible Choice (2003)
(with Linda Francis)
*In-depth explanation, experiential
learning, and practical applications*

Thoughts from
The Heart of the Soul:
**Meditations for
Emotional Awareness** (2002)

Self-Empowerment
Journal:
**Companion to
The Mind of the Soul** (2003)

Soul to Soul

Communications from the Heart

GARY ZUKAV

FREE PRESS

New York   London   Toronto   Sydney

FREE PRESS
1230 Avenue of the Americas
New York, NY 10020

Copyright © 2007 by Gary Zukav and Linda Francis

All rights reserved,
including the right to reproduce
this book or portions thereof
in any form whatsoever.
For information, address
Free Press Subsidiary Rights Department,
1230 Avenue of the Americas,
New York, NY 10020

First Free Press hardcover edition October 2007

FREE PRESS and colophon are
trademarks of Simon & Schuster, Inc.

For information about special discounts for bulk purchases,
please contact Simon & Schuster Special Sales at 1-800-456-6798
or business@simonandschuster.com

Manufactured in the United States of America

10   9   8   7   6   5   4   3   2   1

Library of Congress Cataloging-in-Publication Data

Zukav, Gary.
Soul to soul / Gary Zukav.—1st Free Press hardcover ed.
p.   cm.
1. Spirituality.   2. New Age movement.
3. Spiritual life—New Age movement.   I. Title.
BP605.N48Z8535   2007
204'.32—dc22   2007023482

ISBN-13: 978-0-7432-3700-0
ISBN-10:   0-7432-3700-5

This book is dedicated with love
and appreciation to Linda Francis, my spiritual partner,
playmate, and co-creator.

ACKNOWLEDGMENTS

I am grateful most of all to my guides and Teachers for continual support, whether or not I am listening for it, and to Linda Francis, whose love and wisdom nurture me daily. I am also grateful to the participants in the Authentic Power Program of the Seat of the Soul Institute, whose courage and wisdom humble and inspire me. I am especially grateful to my editor, Frederic W. Hills, whose passion for editorial elegance and books of the heart has shaped this volume into the beautiful reading experience that it is.

Your heart is your home, and all roads lead to home.
—G.Z.

CONTENTS

PART TWO: SOUL QUESTIONS

PART ONE

Soul Subjects

Exploring Soul Subjects

A Soul Subject is not a mental creation. It is an observation. It is a perception that resonates with a deeper part of yourself than the intellect can reach. Not every perception is a Soul Subject. To the five senses—taste, touch, sight, smell, and hearing—a perception is data about the physical world. A Soul Subject is a multisensory perception. It is an observation of physical circumstances plus a recognition of what they mean.

Last week a group of friends met. One of us found a thorn—from a thistle growing along a nearby stream—in the carpet in front of him. I noticed him pondering it as we met. At the end of the meeting he said, "This thorn is the defensive part of a plant. It has been helping me to realize that I am open to people now in ways that I have never been before. I don't need the defenses that I used to have."

That was a Soul Subject. It was more than the perception of a wayward thorn. It was the recognition of a new freedom that had been calling him. How many Soul Subjects have you noticed in your life today? If you are looking, you will see them unfolding before you each moment, like my friend did when he pondered finding a thorn in the carpet—a thorn that no longer defended the plant that grew it.

We live in a world of meaning. That world is the Earth school, the physical arena of our personal and collective experiences. We are the students. Our experiences are the curriculum.

They are our Soul Subjects. Let's explore them now.

Experiencing
the Seasons

BALANCE

When I lived in the city, I never knew what an equinox was. It is an astronomical term for the time when the sun crosses the equator, making night and day of equal length in all parts of the world. In December, the sun is lowest in the sky and the nights are longest. This is the winter solstice. In June, the opposite happens—the sun is highest in the sky and the days are longest. This is the summer solstice. All of this has to do with the equinoxes, but I didn't learn any of it by studying astronomy.

I was forty-five when I moved onto a remote ranch in the pine and fir of northern California. I lived alone. The nearest town was fifteen miles away. I had no electricity or phone. When I returned from infrequent trips, I would get out of my car and stand still for several minutes, listening to the sounds of the evening, and of the stream behind the house. When I walked toward the house, the noise of my boots on the cinder seemed so loud that it startled me.

Winter came, then spring, summer, and fall again. I lived a complete cycle with nature, for the first time. I saw how the sun moved from north to south and back again, and from low in the sky to high, and then down again. I saw the grass in the meadows turn from green to brown, and then disappear under the snow. I saw the stream freeze, thaw, and run freely again with butterflies playing over it.

More important, I felt the seasons come and go inside me.

That is how I learned about the equinoxes. They are midway between the times when the sun is highest (in the summer) and when it is lowest (in the winter). The days are not overly long or overly short. We call the equinoxes spring and fall.

In the United States, the spring equinox, also called the vernal equinox, comes in the month of March. Farmers and gardeners plant crops and all of us relax into the warming weather. Everywhere south of the equator, it is the fall equinox. Farmers and gardeners are harvesting and everyone is preparing for winter.

Do you see the perfect balance? Day and night, spring and fall, hot and cold, planting and harvesting—everything is balanced at the equinoxes. This balance could not exist without the extremes. Midway between the heat of summer and the ice of winter, between sowing and reaping, between darkness and light, life goes on. That is now.

When you strive for balance, be gentle with yourself. How can you recognize balance without recognizing imbalance? When you rejoice at the good that you discover in yourself, or despair at the evil, do you move past the balance point between them without noticing it? If you strive only to avoid the darkness or to cling to the light, you cannot live in balance. Instead, try striving to be conscious of all that you are, and to choose responsibly at each moment.

That is balance.

SPRING TRUST

In the northern hemisphere, where I live, it is spring. Blossoms are blooming on the fruit trees and leaves are budding. Everyone is relieved that the winter is over at last. Why speak of trust when everything is becoming fresh anew, vibrant, and wondrous?

It is not only things going wrong that frighten us. It is also our lives going profoundly right. It is clarity piercing the armor of encrusted prejudices—about others and ourselves. It is new vitality sweeping away the stagnation of lethargy. It is deep roots, long buried beneath the surface, sending up sprouts to at last burst uncontrolled into sunlight.

That sunlight is your consciousness. The birth of new life is as challenging as it is exhilarating, as frightening as it is liberating. Are you prepared to leave old fears, angers, and judgments behind? Are you willing to see yourself as endlessly creative, and responsible for what you create?

Spiritual growth is not an easy escape from the painful circumstances of your life. It begins with an eyes-open exploration of them and their cause. You are the cause. Every insight that brings you to this realization is a springtime—a new beginning. Every impulse to follow your heart is a springtime, too. As you move away from the familiar orientation of being a victim of circumstance to the new, accurate understanding of yourself as a powerful creator, you leave behind the familiar props upon which you once depended. These are your righteous judgments, unchallenged beliefs, and feelings of superiority or inferiority. You are in new territory. The old is gone and everything that is emerging is new.

That is what is happening now, in the spring. No one doubts that new grass growing in the spring is a miracle. Everyone can see that flowers blooming in the spring are miracles. Can you see yourself that way when new insights cause you to question old values? Can you see yourself as blooming when old goals fall away and new, surprising aspirations require you to change your life?

You cannot grow spiritually and remain the same. Understanding that is knowledge. Seeing it is wisdom.

Knowing it is trust.

THE SUMMER SOLSTICE

One special day in June the sun is higher in the sky than it is at any other time of the year. That day is also the longest day of the year. It is the summer solstice. Maximal potential and maximal growth are happening together. The spring gives way to the full force of summer, but the harvest is still months away.

When I lived on my ranch I felt most at ease during the summer. I had no fires to build, no pipes to thaw, no snow to shovel, and I knew that I had months until the fall to lay away the firewood that would keep me warm in the winter. A friend down the road had a black Arabian stallion named Darshan. Each summer I let him graze in my meadow. The split cedar fence, laid into place decades before my arrival and enclosing three acres of grass and wildflowers, seemed to me the perfect place for this magnificent animal, and apparently he felt that way, too. As the summer stretched before me, I lost track of the winter behind me and the winter ahead. I walked the stream in the hot afternoons and jogged old logging roads in the cool of the morning. I repaired the generator, cleaned the wooden water tank in the old barn, and wrote my book. Surrounded by thousands of acres of timberland, I soaked in the heat and the vitality of the summer and immersed myself in them undisturbed.

The fall approached almost imperceptibly. The heat of September days gave way to the coolness of September nights and I began to appreciate again the warm clothing I had put away and forgotten so long ago, at the beginning of the summer. Perhaps because I gave myself to the summer I was ready for the fall, and because I gave myself to the fall, I was ready for the winter when it arrived again, too. As the year completed itself and another began, the summer became more to me than the beautiful season of warmth and light that I love so much. It became part of a larger picture that I began to love even more than its many parts. I didn't realize it at the time, but my awareness was expanding beyond my limited perception of the summer to a larger perspective of the cycle that contains and produces summers, and beyond my limited perception of my life to the larger perspective of the soul that generates and utilizes lifetimes.

Honor the insights that appear in you the same way. As the seasons of your life come and go, acknowledge the shifts that happen in you and allow them to mature in their own time. Don't think of yourself as hypocritical because you aren't living the fullness of your vision immediately. The limitations of your perception are already giving way to a larger perspective in which your struggles are a part of the goal you are striving for and inseparable from it. The fullness of your most noble and healthy aspirations will come, just like the fall harvest always comes. The harvest and the sprouts do not occur together. First come the sprouts, then growth and maturation, and then the harvest.

Let wisdom and love sprout and grow in you the same way.

And enjoy the solstice.

THE WINTER SOLSTICE

In the hemisphere where I live, the deepest moment of the winter comes not in January or February, but in December, when the night is longest and the day is shortest. This day and night is, as we have said, called the winter solstice. It is the mirror image of the summer solstice in June when the day is longest and the night is shortest.

The winter solstice is a very powerful time in the cycle of life and death, death and rebirth, disintegration and renewal that controls all Life on the Earth, including you. It is the time when motion ceases and at the same moment, Life begins to stir again. Animals in hibernation and seeds in sleep beneath the snow will not move until the spring, but deep within them a process has completed itself. The contraction of energy that the long nights and cold days reflect reaches its limit and a cycle reverses itself. From that moment forward, even though the winter remains to unfold as it must, the spring has been born, and the summer, and the harvests of the summer will follow with it.

This dark and trying season is repeated in your life again and again. Each tragedy, loss, failure, and humiliation reaches its inmost movement, spends its energy, and from that long journey another begins—a journey to warmth, light, and expansion. The season of celebration, of growth, of Life, and of movement is repeated again in the same way. One season follows the other.

The arrival of one signals the coming of the other. They do not exist apart.

These seasons of the year, and seasons of your life, come and go, complete themselves, and give way to each other whether you are aware of the dynamic that controls them or not. If you are not, the seasons appear to have lives of their own and you forget they are each part of a cycle—a cycle that you have encountered many times before and will encounter many times again. Your life is built on this cycle of seasons—on the continual repetition of them. The arrival of winter, the coming of darkness and death, initiates the coming of light and life. This cycle controls the unfolding of your life and all within it.

When you are aware of this cycle, you can participate with it. You cannot stop the death that comes in the winter nor the life that comes with the summer, but you can determine in the winter what will be born in the summer. You can contribute your intelligence and will to the intelligence and movement of a dynamic larger than you. You can plant the seed that will sprout in the spring. You can lay the foundation for a different winter to come after the summer that has yet to arrive. You can only do this for yourself.

When you are in deep winter, the nights are long and the days are short. The Earth grows cold and life retreats. Now is the time for you to awaken to your place in this cycle, and to use it consciously. What is darkest in your life? What loss or disappointment, fear or terror moves through you? What powerlessness haunts you? These are given to you for your benefit. They are brought to your awareness so that you can change them. They are your avenues to the clarity and love that you are waiting for. You cannot become fearless at your command, but you can determine how you will respond to your fear. You cannot become kind with one intention, but you can determine how you will respond to your own brutality, righteousness, and fear.

This is the power of the deep winter. It challenges you, confronts you, and shows you what you must change in yourself. It is a holy and precious season. It illuminates your holy and precious life. It is your potential beckoning to you, disguised as an adversary, a tragedy, or a disaster. Will the adversary, tragedy, or disaster shape your experience, or will you shape your experience of it? Will your fears overwhelm you, or will they show you new and different ways to respond to them?

What new life is stirring in you this Deep Winter?

Understanding Love

UNDYING LOVE

My adopted Sioux uncle tells me, "Nephew, life is like a buffalo's breath on a cold winter day. It is there," he says, straightening the fingers of his wrinkled hand, "and then it's gone," curling them into a ball again. Life comes and goes like the cloud of a moist breath on a frosty morning.

My father's life began in 1914 and ended in 1999. He lived through the Depression, raised a family, and gave me my most valuable lessons. He didn't do that by telling me things, although he tried. I disagreed with most of what he said. He did it by loving me through our darkest times together, even while he lay mortally ill. Eventually, I came to love him as much as I discovered that he loved me.

This is the journey that all of us are on—the journey from Love to Love. What happens between the beginning and the end of the journey is your life. I was with my father during his last days in the Earth school. Not even a brain hemorrhage could stop the love that radiated from him. Nothing could. It was not a love that depended on words or actions, or even thoughts. This is the love that we come from and the love that we are going toward. It is also the love that we are.

My father stepped into that love while he was still in the Earth school, immobilized in a hospital bed. It transformed him and everyone around him. He is no longer in the Earth school but that love is. It is in you and it is in me. What would it be like to live a life in that love? Some of us have. Our religions are named after them.

Now it is our turn.

THE CURRENCY OF THE HEART

It was more than a month since my father died in his bed in room 309. Many more patients and their families had filled that room and, like us, moved on. The nurses who comforted us so tenderly, cared for us so professionally, and, in some cases, cried with us, still went from room to room on the hour. The aides who followed them still did the same. The sweet woman who mopped the floor each day still mopped. They touched our lives so deeply but we scarcely had time to thank them. After the hospital came the funeral home and then a house without father.

Now my mother greeted the head nurse again, this time with gifts for her and her staff. Small-town people know each other, even if at a distance. My mother had known this woman since she was an infant, and played bridge with her mother for almost that long.

"You gave us more than we gave you," said the nurse, a brusque horsewoman not accustomed to speaking softly.

She paused and continued. "You let us grieve with you. Families who come here usually keep us at a distance, and sometimes that makes us feel as if something is wrong with us. You let us share your grief with you, and so we could share your love with you, too."

We never thought about hiding our love for Dad, and they never thought about hiding their love for us. We grieved the loss of his vitality, and then his life, and they did, too. We celebrated

his life, and they felt that, also. They were with us through difficult and wondrous times, and we were with them. We witnessed
the miracle of life and death together. Now we are joined by what
we shared.

What we shared was real. Nothing else can bond humans.
Joy, sorrow, care, courage, and tenderness are real. Kindness is
real. Tears are real, and so is laughter. These are the currency of
the heart.

They are meant to be exchanged.

DEEP CHRISTMAS

Christmas is a season of active love. Your life in the Earth school is meant to be a season of active love, but at Christmas those of us in Christian parts of the world see this more clearly than at other times. We feel warm toward others, appreciative of others, and kind. When this experience comes, we feel more alive and connected. We are part of the season and the season is part of us. When it goes, life is flatter, less interesting, less exciting, and less fulfilling.

Active love goes beyond warm feelings and connected moments. It is looking for what is needed and providing it. It is living directly from the heart without reservation. It is realizing that what you see needs to be done is for you to do.

This realization has nothing to do with the exchange of gifts or good wishes. It is the fullness of your life coming to meet you. It is the end of waiting for others to give what you want to give, others to say what you want to say, and others to do what you want to do. It is leaving behind expectations of acknowledgment, praise, and appreciation. It is honoring your inner sense of appropriateness and committing the full force of your being to it.

The shallow giving and receiving of gifts and best wishes is replaced with the deep gratification of knowing that you belong to Life. You are bonded to your fellow students in the Earth school by your love for Life, your commitment to Life, and your joy of Life.

This season does not end with the new year. It does not end with a new century, a new millennium, or a new astrological cycle. It never ends. It is the celebration of all that you are, recognized in others and the world that you are creating together.

When that is a world of harmony, cooperation, sharing, and reverence for Life, you step into the power and consciousness of Christmas—the deep Christmas that you were born to celebrate, moment by moment, decision by decision.

IN HIS WALLET

Every year the high school in my small town welcomes its freshman class with a special retreat. Those who are willing spend a day and a half in a rural setting, playing outdoor games, sharing their talents, and going as deep with each other and themselves as they desire.

The results are impressive. The grade point average at this school is above the state average and the dropout rate is half. Not all students come and some come grudgingly. In groups of a hundred they interact with each other and with upperclassmen, and through their interactions they learn that the bond that can take them through the next four years, and beyond if they choose, is love. They are not taught that with words, but they experience it, and once they do they cannot pretend that love does not exist.

In circles of ten or twelve on the second day, for example, each writes on a small piece of paper what he or she values in the other members of the group. First everyone writes about one person in the circle. Then they each read aloud to that person what they wrote. The person listening is allowed only three responses: "Thank you," or "Thank you very much," or "Thank you—will you read that again." Then they write about a second person, and so on.

They look for something fundamental to value. Not, for example, an ability such as, "You are a wonderful athlete," and not a characteristic such as, "You are so charming," but something meaningful such as, "I appreciate how you take strong stands without making people wrong," and "I feel safe around you because I know you are listening."

A few years ago a graduate of this high school was killed in a traffic accident. In his wallet were small pieces of paper from the beginning of his freshman year with words of appreciation written by new friends in a circle of peers.

What can you say to someone that is so meaningful that he will carry it with him unto death? Only a message from the heart can reach that deep, heal that powerfully, and last that long.

How many messages from your heart have you shared today?

EXCEPT LOVE

A friend told me of an experience she had in the hospital on her way to surgery. As she lay terrified on the dolly being rolled toward the operating room, an orderly appeared by her side and quietly took her hand. She believes he was male, but the fear she felt clouds her memory. The orderly walked beside her down the hall, into an elevator, out, and down another hall. Her terror began to subside. When they reached the operating room, he gently released her hand and she was rolled in. She was still frightened, but the feeling of being cared for by an unrecognized friend filled more of her mind than her fear. With the warmth of his hand still in hers, she was anesthetized.

When she awoke in her room, the surgery successful, all she recalled was that hand in hers and the safe and cared-for way she felt.

"I don't remember the color of his skin or anything about him," she said softly, "but I will always remember that act of compassion."

My friend will remember that act long after she has forgotten most of the events in her life. What made that experience so special? Can you imagine caring enough about a stranger to comfort her with the touch of your hand? Can you feel the fear of others, and meet it with kindness?

Love is feeling the pain of others as if it were your own, and acting accordingly. Restricting your love to your family, or to those you know, or those who look, think, act, dress, and speak like you prevents you from experiencing your ability to love. It is unlimited. You cannot experience the vastness of your ability to love by loving in moderation. You do not need to hug everyone you meet, but your heart can be open. You do not need to converse with each stranger, but your heart can be open. Openness to others as you would like others to be open to you is love. The orderly in my friend's life opened himself to her, and she will never forget him.

Can you live with an open heart, even while others are frightened? Love is not taking advantage of the vulnerabilities of others. It is making the needs of others as important as your own. Love is a fire that is out of control. Once ignited, it cannot be contained. You may strive for moderation in diet, exercise, and work hours, but striving for moderation in love is like striving for moderation in breathing.

Practice moderation in all things except love.

Challenging Your Fears

SNAKE SKIN

We had gathered from around the country and Canada for a retreat. Each participant had come with gifts to give, questions to ask, challenges to present, and solutions to offer.

We began as we usually do—with a check-in. We sat in a circle and, one by one, offered what we were moved to share, or remained silent. At last a woman from Canada with a solid quality about her spoke.

"Last week I found a snake skin on the road. I stopped and brought it home. It was perfectly preserved. I put it in my window and during the following days I looked at it again and again. I knew that in some way it was a big part of my life, but it wasn't until I came here that I understood how.

"I am usually scared to fly, but this time I wasn't frightened! The flight was actually pleasant for me. I thought about that on my way from the airport to here, and I have been thinking about it for the last few days.

"I miss my fear. I keep looking around for it because it is so familiar. There is a huge openness in me now where the fear used to be. I don't know yet what to do with it."

Fear becomes comfortable, even though it is painful, if it stays long enough. So do anger, jealousy, greed, and vengefulness. They begin to appear as old friends. You know how to relate to them and after a while you feel uncomfortable when they are not present. The old skin feels natural because you have worn it a long time.

Our friend's snake skin was perfectly preserved, and she put it on her windowsill in honor of what it meant to her. You can shed your perfectly preserved anger, jealousy, hatred of yourself or others, greed, and every other painful emotion just like the snake shed its skin. Eventually, you will. When you finally make the connection between these emotions and the pain in your life, you will change. Until then, you will spend your energy and time on the Earth trying to change others.

Knowing that your painful emotions are designed to bring your attention to the parts of your personality that you were born to challenge and change accelerates this process—the process of transforming yourself from an angry, jealous, avaricious, or vengeful person into one who is compassionate, wise, and grateful for Life.

As you begin to move in this direction, your old ways of thinking, perceiving, and acting will call to you. Put them in your window, where the light is greatest, and appreciate them.

Then move forward.

THE OTHER SIDE OF THE COIN

Linda and I were midway through a workshop on emotional awareness. I had given an example from my life in which I thought, at the time, that I was aware of what I was feeling but, in retrospect, was not.

This was the example: When I graduated from college I yearned to join the military. I feared that the Vietnam War would be over before I could participate in it. I enlisted in the infantry, then went to infantry Officer Candidate School where I became an infantry officer, then volunteered for jump school where I became a paratrooper, and, at last, volunteered for the Special Forces (Green Berets). After all that volunteering, I went to Vietnam as the executive officer of a twelve-man detachment called an "A team."

Our mission was Top Secret. Our weapons were Top Secret. We wore special uniforms, drove special vehicles, and received special support, such as special aircraft and Top Secret intelligence. I was proud of what I was doing because I thought it was very masculine. I liked my uniform. I liked my boots, beret, and weapons. I felt superior to the rest of the Army because of what I did.

I considered myself to be brave because I did things that scared me, such as parachuting at night, riding in helicopters, and shooting at people who were shooting at me. It never occurred to me that I was a frightened person. If someone had said to me, "You are a Green Beret officer and you do the things that you do because you are frightened," I would not have believed it. I would have exploded with anger.

That could have been my first clue—anger at the suggestion that I was frightened—but I did not know enough in those days to look for it. I thought I was courageous at the time, but in retrospect I realized that I did not have the courage to face how frightened I was of being rejected, of trying and failing, and of not living up to my expectations and the expectations of others. These fears were intensely painful, and I avoided feeling them by doing dangerous and, to me, manly things.

It was only years later that I could recognize how frightened I was. I thought I knew what I was feeling at that time, but I did not. I needed to be admired, to be doing things that I felt were admirable, and to justify my anger. The more frightened I became, the more angry I became, and the more daring became the things that I volunteered for. I knew that I was angry but I did not realize how frightened I was.

There was a long silence in the room. A quiet man a few rows in front of me began to nod his head slowly, and then he spoke.

"During the time you were in Vietnam," he began, "I burned my draft card and marched twice on Washington."

He paused for a moment. "I was at war with the government the same way you were at war in Vietnam. I was angry the same way that you were angry. I was also frightened and not able to see how frightened I was.

"You and I took the same journey," he continued. "It just looked different."

The journey was from emotional avoidance to emotional awareness, from victimhood to responsibility, and from anger to compassion. It was a journey that required courage, and we shared it—two brothers who arrived at the same place in their own ways, in their own time.

We are all on the same journey. We do not have the choice to take the journey or not. We have only the choices of when we will begin the journey and how we will treat ourselves and each other along the way.

THE ASSUMPTION

A acquaintance I had not seen in months called on Christmas to say hello. The voice that answered asked his name, told him to wait, and then returned to say that no one by that name was known to her. Crushed by this message, my acquaintance wondered what he could have done to anger me or Linda, what insensitivity he had unknowingly displayed, or which of his inadequacies we might have discovered.

Linda and I met him on a walk a month later. He tentatively mentioned his experience. "You must have called the wrong number," we assured him, but he was certain that was not the case. He was correct. When we followed him into his house and found the number, it was that of our assistant. "I thought so," he said, now certain that he had been rejected.

Only when we assured him that our assistant did not work on Christmas and that a substitute was filling in for her did he realize the anguish he experienced had not been necessary. We were still glad to see him, and we were not sending him covert signals to the contrary. We stayed to discuss a similar incident the year prior, in which he interpreted one of our actions in the same way—as a rejection.

"This is a reaction—feeling rejected—that you have felt with other people also, isn't it?" I asked him. He agreed, and our first genuine conversation began.

"I have been struggling with my feelings of unworthiness for years," said Linda. "When they come now, I recognize them, so even though they are painful, I don't act on them."

"How could *you* have feelings of unworthiness?!" he asked, unbelievingly, of Linda. "You are so composed and focused. You are so warm and welcoming!"

Linda assured him that she had indeed challenged those very feelings, and continued to challenge them.

"I am so relieved," he sighed, "that I am not the only one to feel this horrible about myself."

Linda's feelings of unworthiness, our friend's, and yours are no different. That painful experience lies at the heart of human experience. It is the pain of not being good enough, attractive enough, or human enough. It is the fear of being seen for who you really are, and rejected. These are experiences of powerlessness. They are tormenting anguishes that drive you to please other people, dominate other people, shop when you do not need to buy anything, eat when you are not hungry, take drugs, drink alcohol, have mindless sex, feel inferior, feel superior, and countless other activities to make yourself feel safe and lovable. In this case, our acquaintance had withdrawn into feelings of inferiority. If we had not met him on our walk he would have stayed there—and grown more and more distant from Linda and me.

What emotional reaction controls your thoughts and perceptions when you feel powerless—unloved and unlovable? Is it disdain and superiority, emotional withdrawal, jealousy, rage, or fear? Your painful emotional reactions may or may not have anything to do with the person who triggers them, just as the reaction of our acquaintance had nothing to do with Linda or me. It had everything to do with him. Your emotional reactions have everything to do with you. When they come, you can observe them instead of acting on them. You do not need to speak angrily merely because you are angry, or attempt to please someone because you feel the need to please him.

Instead of attempting to change someone else to make yourself feel better, you can change yourself. Instead of assuming what makes you feel worst, assume what makes you feel the best. You are free to make the most positive assumption as well as the most negative.

Imagine that you are worthy and valuable, precious and loved. How does that assumption make you feel?'

LIKE AN ARROW

During the High Holy Days, Jews participate in a ten-day examination of their actions and thoughts over the past year and end this process with a special, holy day of prayer. On that day—knowing what they want to change in themselves—they set their intentions to change. Each looks for occasions when he or she strayed from his or her pure soul. They hold the image of their lives during the past year as an arrow that was heading toward this target, identify what deflected the arrow, and then intend to change it. A rabbi explained it to me this way, "We use the word *sin* to mean 'missing the mark' and on the special day that completes this process of introspection, we put ourselves back on track."

Creating authentic power—the alignment of your personality with your soul—requires discovering the parts of your personality that are creating destructive consequences and changing them. As you do that, you put your life on a trajectory toward your greatest potential—a life of harmony, cooperation, sharing, and reverence for Life, which is a life of meaning and joy. You allow the arrow to find its mark by removing the influences that deflect it. They are your experiences of fear, such as anger, jealousy, vengefulness, and every other painful emotion. The magnetic field of fear calls to you every day. It is the need to be right or righteous, to make other people wrong, to criticize, overeat, buy what you do not need, misuse drugs, or have another drink, among many other things. It is every obsessive, compulsive, and addictive impulse.

You can look for your particular experiences of fear every day and challenge the frightened parts of your personality by not choosing what they want to do—such as shout, withdraw emotionally, or blame the Universe or others for your unpleasant experiences. You can correct the trajectory of the arrow at any time. Once you develop this habit, you will be able to correct the trajectory continually and your life will become a full-time examination of your thoughts and actions and the intention to move toward your highest potential instead of indulging your inadequacies.

Just as Christians do not strive to live the ideals of the Christ only at Christmas, Jews do not strive toward their pure souls only during their highest holy days. They use those days to remind themselves that they are responsible for the trajectory of the arrow.

Are you satisfied with the trajectory of your arrow?

SEVENTY-FIVE PERCENT

A friend of mine owns a small hotel on the Oregon coast. One evening she noticed a group of older men dining together in the restaurant and asked them who they were. Each had been in the same parachute battalion in World War II and, because one of them lived in the same town as my friend's hotel, they were having their annual reunion there that year.

My friend, who is not shy, joined them immediately. "What did it look like to do what you did in World War II?" she asked them, drawing up a chair. "What did it smell like? What did it taste like?" and the following story unfolded.

Seventy-five percent of their battalion was killed the day they parachuted into combat. They had prepared a long time for their jump and in that time they had talked a lot about different ways they might be killed, such as, "My parachute won't open and I will be killed; the plane will be shot down and I will be killed; I will land in a tree and be killed; I will be shot in the drop zone and be killed; I will be captured and then I will be killed." Their fear was so intense that they needed to sing a song in the plane to give themselves the courage to jump. ("It was a little dirty," my friend said, chuckling.) On the way down they were so frightened that some of them soiled their trousers and others vomited.

My friend listened as one after the other shared memories. "After all that," my friend asked them, "what was the best year in your life?" She thought that question might change the conversation, but instead, all of the men without exception said, "That year!" That year of intense feeling, of intense focus and intense appreciation for Life remained the year that each remembered as his best. "What about the year you got married?" she asked, and "What about the year your children were born?" None of the men changed his answer. That year—the year that three-quarters of the people around them were killed—remained in their opinion the best year of their lives.

If you did nothing else than feel deeply at every moment, think about your life at every moment, and treasure life very much at every moment, wouldn't that be a special time for you, too? It doesn't require a horrible experience or the death of seventy-five percent of the people around you to feel deeply and focus your thoughts on how precious Life is, but whenever you do, your life will become so meaningful to you that you will savor it. You can do that this year.

You can do it now.

The Fork in the Road

MOMENT OF CHOICE

There comes a time when the pain of continuing exceeds the pain of stopping. At that moment, a threshold is crossed. What seemed unthinkable becomes thinkable. Slowly the realization emerges that the choice to continue what you have been doing is the choice to live in discomfort, and the choice to stop what you have been doing is the choice to breathe deeply and freely again. Once that realization has emerged, you can either honor it or ignore it, but you cannot forget it.

This realization puts you into new territory—the territory of self-responsibility. You can no longer blame your discomfort on others. The power to continue or to stop is fully in your hands. Your pain becomes a matter of your own choice. To stop the pain requires changing yourself—changing your need to please or dominate, to be right or wrong, to be strong or weak. At risk is an image you have created and sustained but that no longer serves you—the image of one who is considerate or arrogant, simple or complex, tender or practical. No image of yourself can survive the realization that it is causing you to live in pain and fear.

When you will stop what you are doing is for you to decide. Your need for approval or to push others away may provide you with the only security, or pleasure, that you have. You may not be ready to give up the activities, judgments, and thoughts that are familiar to you. The attraction of pleasing others again, making all well again, shouting louder again, being smarter again, and so on will call to you. At the same time, the new world that you have glimpsed will call to you, also. To step into it requires abandoning an obsolete role.

A friend of mine became uncomfortable with the behavior of an employee. At the same time, he feared losing the service of the employee at a critical time in the development of his business. He spoke to his employee, but the conversation gave him no relief. He tried to rationalize his discomfort, but it continued. He thought of how foolish he would be to dismiss an important employee. He thought of the hardship he would cause the employee. To make the issue more complex, he liked the employee. When he thought of continuing to work with the employee, his chest felt heavy and his stomach hurt. When he thought of working without the employee, he felt lighter and freer.

At last he realized that he must dismiss the employee or continue to live with the discomfort of working with him. To dismiss the employee required him to say no, to draw boundaries, to risk failure as a businessman. To continue required him to remain trapped in his image of himself as sensitive, caring, and generous.

This was his moment of choice.

In the case of my friend, he asked the employee to leave. It was difficult for him, but in the process he discovered different, surprising new definitions of sensitivity, care, and generosity. His sensitivity allowed him to sense what was not working. His care for himself and his employee prevented him from continuing with an unhealthy relationship. His generosity inspired him to sever a mutually dependent bond that inhibited the spiritual development of both.

What is your moment of choice? You do not need to look for

one as dramatic as my friend's. Each moment is a moment of choice—a time to leave the old, the limited, the restrained, and the contracted for the new, the unbounded, and the liberating potential that expands before you. You cannot stop making choices. That is what your moments are for.

COMPASSION OR REVENGE

The attacks on the World Trade Center and the Pentagon are occasions of great significance. They are opportunities for you to feel inside, to find those parts of yourself that are in fear, and to make the decision to move forward in your life without fear. That is the challenge for each individual on this planet today. The pursuit of external power—the ability to manipulate and control—creates only violence and destruction. The painful events in New York and Washington are examples of that reality.

The causal chain that created this violence is one in which compassion and wisdom are absent. Are wisdom and compassion present in you as you watch television and read the newspapers? It is important to realize that you do not know, and cannot know, all that came to conclusion, or into Karmic balance, as a result of these events. Because you are not able to know all that can be known about them, you are not in a position to judge them.

When you are able to look at the events of the Earth school from this perspective, you will see clearly the central importance of the role that you play in it. That role is this: It is for you to decide what you will contribute to this world. Many will be asking your opinion of these events. Each question is an opportunity for you to contribute to the love that is in the world or to the fear that is in the world. This is the same opportunity that presents itself to you at each moment.

If you hate those who hate, you become like them. You add to the violence and the destructive energy that now fills our world. As you make the decision to see with clarity and compassion, you will see that those who committed these acts of violence were in extreme pain themselves, and that they were fueled by the violent parts of ourselves—the parts that judge without mercy, strike in anger, and rejoice in the suffering of others. They were our proxy participants. If you can look with compassion upon those who have suffered and those who have committed acts of cruelty alike, then you will see that all are suffering. The remedy for suffering is not to inflict more suffering.

This is an opportunity for a massive expression of compassion. It is also an opportunity for a massive expression of revenge. Which world do you intend to live in—a world of revenge or a world of compassion?

FIRST SIGHT

There once was a man who had been blind from birth. He had never seen anything but blackness, so he didn't know that there was anything else to see.

One year a new operation was invented to give sight to just the kind of vision defect that this man had.

"I have good news for you," said his doctor. "You will be able to see!"

"What is it like to see?" asked the blind man, because he had never had the experience.

The doctor and all of the man's friends tried to explain what it was like to see, but the blind man could not understand anything that they said. "I don't understand what you mean by green," he would say, or, "What do you mean by stars shining in the sky?"

At last it was clear to everyone, including the blind man, that no one could tell him what it was like to see, but he still had the opportunity of seeing, if he wanted.

He thought about it again and again, and then called his doctor.

"Will I be able to use my cane when I see?" he asked. "I don't want to see if I can't use my cane."

A new life is calling you now. It is the birth of a new species that longs to occur now in each of us. It is an attraction to harmony, cooperation, sharing, and reverence for Life that did not exist before. It is sensing, seeing, feeling, or hearing intelligence, wisdom, and compassion that we were not aware of before.

This new life requires challenging every fear—the fear of being vulnerable, of loving and losing, of being loved and losing, of trying and failing, of being betrayed, of being used, of not having enough, and of having too much. These are our canes. They are all that we have known for most of our lives. They have helped us to navigate through the most difficult times, in the most difficult of worlds. We feel naked without them, even though they hurt.

The life that is calling you has no fear in it. Whether you create that life or not is for you to decide. You do not have to choose harmony, cooperation, sharing, and reverence for Life in your daily struggles, but they are required if you want your new life. You do not have to listen to the wisdom and compassion that are now coming into your consciousness, but you won't be able to create your new life if you don't.

Which will you choose—your new life or your fears?

How important is your cane to you?

LINCOLN TUNNEL

During a trip to New York City, a young woman told Linda and me about her weekend holidays with her husband. "We would return to the City refreshed but, for some reason, we would become irritable with each other before we got home. By the time we were climbing the stairs to our apartment, we were locked in arguments."

After several trips, they both noticed that their interactions began to deteriorate as they drove through the Lincoln Tunnel, the last part of their journey back to Manhattan. "We came to the conclusion," she continued, "that going through the Lincoln Tunnel made us start to think about the week ahead—pressure at work, email to answer, and family matters to attend to." As a result, they lost touch with the relaxation and closeness they had enjoyed over the weekend.

Then she took a very important step. "Now, when we approach the Lincoln Tunnel," she continued with enthusiasm, "we look for stresses that we might be feeling and do whatever is necessary to stay connected." The Lincoln Tunnel has become a reminder for them to pay attention to their emotions and to keep in touch with their love for each other.

"We made a decision," she finished her story, "not to let the pressures we feel determine how we treat each other."

That was a responsible choice—it created consequences for which she was willing to assume responsibility. She was no longer willing to create tension and discord merely because she felt stress. Instead, she chose to create harmony *while she was feeling stress*. The Lincoln Tunnel now reminds her to begin that process or return to it.

Can you recognize when you are creating consequences you do not want, and choose differently, even while you feel the impulse to shout, withdraw emotionally, seek revenge, criticize people in your mind, or any of the other ways that you have created painful consequences in the past? Doing that is at the heart of creating authentic power, and no one else can do it for you.

You can start by choosing differently the next time you feel an irresistible urge to argue, or you are certain that you are right and someone else is wrong. The more you decide for yourself what you will create with your words and actions instead of speaking and behaving as you are accustomed when you are upset, the more you will encounter consequences that you want to experience.

Eventually, every interaction will become a Lincoln Tunnel experience for you.

New Perceptions

NEW EYES

When I leave home I see it with new eyes. What was ordinary becomes special. I see the beauty of it. I am deeply nourished by the flowers, the rocks, the trees, and the water. I admire the lines of our house and the warm feeling it gives. I see what visitors see, and appreciate it with them. The hours, and then minutes, left to me before we leave for the airport are rich and full. I feel my roots. I remember the wild animals that have visited me here. Most of all I appreciate the growing and loving that Linda and I have done here together. I realize how special our home is and how special our lives are.

All of this happens during the brief interval between the time I wake and the time we leave on our trip. The day before I woke in the same bed, walked through the same house, and looked at the same trees, flowers, water, and rocks. I thought I appreciated them, but compared to the richness of my experiences before our departure, I realize I did not. When the car and the plane await me, I see my home and my life in full color. When I live there each day, I see them in black and white.

Linda and I travel often, and so I have this experience often. Each time it surprises me. Now I have begun to imagine occasionally that I am about to leave on a trip so I can see the beauty my daily preoccupations obscure.

Your life is like that. Beauty surrounds you continually. Sometimes you see it only when you are about to leave it. This mini-scene is a reflection of a macro-scene. The macro-scene is the duration between the time you were born and the time you will die. Your daily preoccupations obscure the beauty around you if you do not make the effort to look for it. When the time comes for you to leave the Earth school, when your death is near, you will see more beauty around you than you can imagine. You will appreciate your fellow students and your interactions with them. You will appreciate the people you have loved, those you have disliked, and even those you have barely noticed.

You may think your life has no beauty, but that is not so. When your death is very near, you will see old battles from a new perspective and they will take on new meaning and richness. You will see the challenges and struggles of your friends and your adversaries, and realize they are not so different from your own. You will see how your experiences, even the difficult ones, served you and others. You will see beauty everywhere you look, and you will see it clearly because you are about to leave it.

Why wait until the moment of your death to appreciate the beauty of your life? That moment is approaching more quickly than you think. The end of your time on the Earth is the conclusion of a powerful and awesome experience. You can touch that awe and power now. You do not have to wait until you are about to leave it. The richness and power of your life are available to you now, just as the beauty of my home is available to me now.

Experiment with taking the time to appreciate the beauty of your life before you are about to leave it.

FIRE SEASON

Where I live, it doesn't rain in the summer. Except for the meadows in the mountains, where spring comes in September, the grass is dry, dry pine needles cover forest floors, and dead wood is tinder. When the lightning strikes, nothing can stop the fire.

That is what happened not long ago. Tens of thousands of acres burned. Thick heavy smoke filled our valley and every valley around it. Linda and I drove an hour to find clear air. By the time the smoke thinned, charred trees and blackened soil were all that was left where forests once grew. Many people consider this a tragedy, but it is not. Fires are part of the natural cycle of forests, and of nature. Where an older forest grew, a new forest will rise.

Consciousness is like that. When it ignites, all that was once valuable to you is swept away in the fire. What previously satisfied no longer does. Higher aspirations replace lower. Compassion replaces anger. Patience replaces disdain. Understanding replaces ignorance. Your life changes in deep and fundamental ways, and you cannot stop the fire.

This is not a tragedy any more than the fire in the forest. Where a life of less awareness once unfolded unconsciously, a new and conscious life now emerges. New goals appear, and new ways of relating lead you to them. New satisfactions, never before considered, fulfill in unexpected ways. Meaning pervades all that you do, and joy carries you forward like a leaf on a river.

Your life is no longer yours alone. You are a companion of the Universe. All of Life is your partner and together you create powerfully.

Sometimes this happens when it hasn't rained in a long time—when sorrow, loneliness, and despair fill your days and everything in your life seems brown and dry. It can happen anytime. Your life can explode with potential that had little possibility of developing the day before, if you are open to it.

Every day is fire season.

THE TOURIST

I was recently preparing *The Dancing Wu Li Masters: An Overview of the New Physics* for publication in a new edition. That required reading it more closely than I had in years. While I was enjoying myself, I came upon a story that I had used to illustrate certain aspects of quantum logic.

"During the Lebanese civil war a visiting American was stopped by a group of masked gunmen. One wrong word could cost him his life.

"Are you Christian or Muslim?" they asked.

"I am a *tourist!*" he cried.

Now, twenty-two years after *The Dancing Wu Li Masters* was written, that story still has a special meaning for me. The power of shifting perspective radically has become a central part of my life. The most fundamental shift, and how to create it, is the content of the next book that I wrote, *The Seat of the Soul.* That is the shift in perspective from victim to creator, from an individual who experiences his or her life into an individual who experiments with his or her life. To make that shift requires asking different questions.

The gunmen in the story ask only, "Are you Christian or Muslim?" That was all they could see, and all that they wanted to see. They could as well have asked, "Are you right or wrong?" or "Are you good or bad?" If the tourist had answered the question that he was asked, he could have caused himself trouble, especially since he didn't know whether the gunmen were Christian or Muslim.

When you look at the events of your life and ask yourself, "Was this good or bad?" or "Was this right or wrong?" you do the same thing as the masked gunmen. You also cause yourself unnecessary complications and pain because you are the one who is forced to answer.

From the perspective of your soul, the experiences of your life are neither good nor bad. They are neither just nor unjust. They are what they need to be, given the wisdom of the choices that you have made. They are opportunities for you to learn in the intimacy of your own experience what you have created in the past, and choose to create differently.

If you distract yourself with questions such as "Why me?" and "Why is the universe so unfair?" you will not be able to make the shift in perspective that will allow you to value every experience in your life, and not only those that you approve.

Until you make that shift, you will feel lucky when events occur as you want them to occur and unfortunate when they do not. Either way, you will see yourself as a victim—sometimes blundering into good fortune and sometimes into bad luck. You will see the universe as capricious, judgmental, and dangerous.

When you see your life as a learning opportunity in which you are provided with continually updated class material that is uniquely suited to your needs, you will see your life as a gift that is worthy of your value and close attention. You will also begin to see the Universe as a wise and compassionate partner in your educational process, and you will be grateful for it.

You will make this shift in perspective sooner or later. You were born to make it. If you do not make it in this lifetime, you will make it in another. The first step toward this shift is to ask yourself after each experience, "What can I learn from this?" rather than "What is right with this?" and "What is wrong with this?"

That is a step that you can take now.

WEARING THE SWORD

In certain European societies it was once expected of gentlemen to wear a sword as a part of formal dress. There is a story of one gentleman who was truly gentle. Today we would call him a compassionate pacifist. By birth he was noble and expected to wear his sword, but wearing it was difficult for him. He was torn between his distaste for violence and the necessity to wear a weapon in order to be well dressed. Not wearing a sword in his society would be the equivalent today of wearing a suit without the coat.

As his distress developed, he consulted an old and trusted friend.

"What can I do?" he asked. "I am uncomfortable wearing my sword and I am uncomfortable not wearing it. Neither is appropriate for me."

"You will wear the sword," replied his friend, "until you are more uncomfortable wearing it than you are uncomfortable not wearing it."

As you develop new awareness, your values change. When that happens, you become uncomfortable expressing yourself in old ways and pursuing old goals. You become uncomfortable with old friends. When you enact your new values and perceptions, you are uncomfortable. When you do not, you are uncomfortable.

This is natural. Waking up to your humanity in a world that considers life a cheap commodity creates challenges that did not exist before. Striving for cooperation while competition is treasured creates challenges. So does sharing instead of hoarding, and contributing to Life instead of exploiting it.

Millions of individuals now face these challenges. These challenges take countless forms. One individual struggles with his need to support a family and his conflicting need to leave a job that suffocates him. Another struggles to express her emotions in a family that is frightened of emotions. In every case, discomfort with what was and discomfort with what is emerging create a tension.

This is the creative tension. It is prelude to a leap from the old to the new. It is the experience of a birth in process. The decision is always whether to release what stands in the way. What stands in the way is all that has given you a sense of security and value. It is the need to meet the expectations of others and fear of the unknown.

Once this creative tension appears, it will intensify until you come to terms with it.

What swords are you wearing?

ALL UPHILL

Years ago, Linda, my spiritual partner, ran a footrace in the mountains near San Diego, California. She remembers that race because of the frustration that she felt at the beginning of it and what happened after that.

The course began with a long uphill grade. Then it continued with another uphill segment. After half an hour, she began to be angry. "When will this course go downhill?" she asked herself. She became more and more upset as she came around every curve and saw that the road continued upward.

"What goes up must come down!" she told herself. When the course did not come down, she began to fume. "It's not fair! For every uphill segment there should be a downhill segment!" There was not. Up and up she ran.

That is when Linda had an insight that changed her life. She still remembers that race because of it. "The course is not going to go downhill. It is all uphill!"

Her fight was over. Her longing for a downhill segment fell away. She no longer raged against the injustice of more uphill than downhill. She was free to do what she came to do—run the race.

"Once I accepted the course the way that it actually was—all uphill—instead of the way I thought it should be—a downhill segment for every uphill segment—I was able to finish the race feeling good about it and myself."

Linda freed energy that had been locked in her as anger and resentment and used that energy to run her race.

Do you resent the injustices in your life? Do you rage against the unfairness of your experiences? Do you long for circumstances to be other than they are?

What would you rather do—resist your life or live it? Linda decided to run her race instead of resisting it. When she did, she began to enjoy herself and the race—even though it was all uphill. Her experience changed from frustration, resentment, and anger into pleasure, joy, and appreciation. The course did not change. Linda did. Because of her change, she ran better and took pleasure in it.

What races are you running, and how much are you resisting them?

THE JOURNEY

Last week I saw a picture in a newspaper of an old lady in failing health. Her body was bloated and her skin was sallow. Her beloved leaned over her weak form, stroking her gray hair and puffy cheeks. Her life support system, a drip tube, hung by her side. In a small box, inserted as a picture within a picture, was another photo of her taken forty years ago. Her skin was flawless, her face elegant and refined, and her eyes sparkled like the diamond necklace that she wore with her evening gown. She was a dazzling female to tens of millions of movie watchers. Her name was a symbol of feminine beauty and sexuality. In the transient world of entertainment, she had appeared like a comet, blazing across the night sky and illuminating the imagination of so many who longed to be famous, elegant, wealthy, and a symbol. She had disappeared almost as quickly.

Now she lay in a hospital, approaching the end of a life that began long before she became a celluloid comet. Who was this person in the photo? The old and bloated lady, or the elegant actress with the perfect face and body? How much more did her life have to offer than the photos beneath the headline announcing that she was close to death? Who made this journey from infancy to adulthood to old age to the hospital with her beloved caressing her cheek? He also was old.

The journey you are on is deep and powerful. Your roots go far below the surface of your appearances. Your infancy, childhood, adulthood, and old age are phases in the development of a plant. The root that produced the plant has produced other plants in the past, and will produce more plants in the future. That root is your soul. The plant is your life. The plant grows, withers, and dies. The root remains. Children do not know about roots. They see plants sprout, grow, and die, and they think that all has gone and will not return. Then they see other plants grow in the spring and die in the fall. Soon they understand roots. They realize that the root is more than the plant.

When you see that your soul is more than your life, you do not confuse the two. You know the plant will wither and die, and you know the root will remain. When you think you are the plant, you cling to each moment of your life and you fear your death. When you know you are the root, you appreciate each moment of your life and you do not fear the withering and death of the plant. When the plant dies, the root begins the process of sprouting another plant. That process will not be apparent until the spring and, if you do not remember the root beneath the surface of the Earth, you will forget that the new plant in the spring comes from the same root as the plant last summer. If you do not remember your soul, your death will appear catastrophic and final. You will think that your birth began your story and your death ends it.

No photo can show your soul. It can show only your appearance at the time it is taken. Your appearances change, but they are not your soul. The old lady in the hospital and her beloved can be photographed, but their souls cannot. When you think the photo in the newspaper reveals who they are, you cannot appreciate the depth and power of the journey they are on, or the depth and power of the journey you are on.

Ask yourself, "Who is on this journey?" when you look into a mirror. Each year you will see changes in the image that asks. Each year you will feel, if you are open to it, changes in the one who journeys. Are you more flexible than last year, or more rigid? Do you think more about your own needs than last year, or more about the needs of others? When your heart softens, you will see the image in the mirror, and the photos of people in newspapers, with appreciation and awe. You will see your own life the same way.

SIX CARS

During an intense snowstorm that shut down the airport for two days and stranded thousands of motorists, six cars were snowbound on a freeway off-ramp near Denver. The weather was brutally cold and death by freezing was a very real possibility if help did not arrive. Instead of remaining in their cars, burning precious fuel to stay warm until it was gone, the six drivers congregated in one car and remained in it until the fuel level went down to one-quarter of a tank. Then they moved to the next car and did the same thing. When a snowplow finally freed them, all were safe and warm and all had enough fuel to find a motel until they could return home.

I have been thinking about that news story ever since I read it, contrasting the alternative possible realities of separation in their suffering and a slow death by freezing for each of six fellow students in the Earth school with the reality they chose to create of connection and common warmth. In myth and some schools of dream analysis, a vehicle, such as a chariot, wagon, or, in modern terms, an automobile, often symbolizes an individual consciousness, the orientation of a personality as it moves through its experiences and that shapes its understanding of them. For example, some individuals see the world as merciless and uncaring while others see it as wise and compassionate, and they have different experiences of the events of their lives as a result. Some see themselves as isolated and forever separate and others see relatives wherever they look, and they, also, have different experiences.

These six drivers not only got out of their respective automobiles, they each shared the automobiles of the others. Symbolically, they each left their habitual consciousness behind in order to support one another, and each visited the consciousness of the others. As a result, they created a new reality that all of them shared and none of them could deny—they got a new "lease on life."

Now I use this story to remind myself that I can get out of my car—leave my old way of seeing and understanding behind, even if only for a while—and get into the car of another individual, and another's, and another's. I need not remained trapped—snowbound—in my habitual way of thinking, judging, blaming, and feeling that I am a victim of my experiences—unless I choose to freeze alone. I can give myself a new "lease on life"—my own life.

Have you suffered in isolation, frozen alone, and ignored the suffering and fear of others because you were suffering and frightened? Do you still? You can use this story, too, to remind yourself of when it is time to get out of your car.

The Art of Letting Go

STANDING IN THE CENTER

When I replaced the wood-burning stove in my house, I had to replace the chimney, too. The new chimney was a stainless-steel tube that fitted inside the old brick chimney.

I hired a workman to do the job and I agreed to help.

"Throw me the pliers," he shouted down.

He was standing on the narrow top of the old brick chimney, almost thirty feet above the ground. If he tried to reach too far and lost his balance, he would fall. Below him was a rocky path.

"Let me bring them up," I suggested.

"Throw them up," he shouted again, as though reading my mind. "I'm an Iroquois Indian. We build skyscrapers. I'm not going to reach too far."

I held my breath and tossed. The pliers sailed upward in a graceful arc toward him. His legs didn't move. His waist didn't move. His chest, shoulders, and head didn't move, either. Only his left arm moved. My throw was good and his hand closed around the pliers.

"Nice toss!" he grinned.

If the pliers had been farther than he could have reached, I knew that he would have let them fall. Even if they had brushed the tips of his fingers, I knew that he would still have let them fall.

Tool after tool sailed up—screwdrivers, a drill bit, and another pair of pliers. Some of them fell. Others didn't. It depended upon how well I could throw, not on how far he could reach. He reached as far as he could, but no farther. My job was to get the tool within his range. When I did, he caught it. When I didn't, it fell.

How far do you reach for security and appreciation? How often do you experience the pain of disappointment, the agony of not getting what you very much want, or of getting what you very much do not want?

Every expectation is a reach too far. Every fall is a lesson. Eventually, you will learn the art of letting whatever is beyond your reach remain there, no matter how appealing or important it appears. Even if it is something you desperately need, even if it is something you long for, even if it is something you think you cannot live without.

When that happens, you will stand in your center, no matter what comes sailing toward you, or how close or how far away it is.

FIGHT OR FLOW

For thirteen years I lived in a small cabin in the woods at the base of a fourteen-thousand-foot volcanic mountain. The tall trees, the animals, and the energy of the volcano filled my life from morning to night. At night I dreamed about them.

I arrived with a broken foot, those many years ago. Hobbling on crutches, I had no choice but to accept the help of my new neighbors. I had furniture to unload and I couldn't walk across the room and drink coffee at the same time. So I watched as they worked, talking with each other and welcoming me into their warm embrace of smiles and sweat as they moved everything I had from the truck.

When I tried to help, one of them said sternly, "Sit down. We'll take care of this." And they did.

For the next one and a third decades I grew with these people, inwardly and outwardly. Now the time had come to move again. Linda and I had lived together in the cabin for seven years. It was too small for us, and we both knew it. Finding a new place wasn't easy, but we made it an adventure. We decided not to envision our new home, and not to limit ourselves with expectations or burden ourselves with our likes and dislikes.

"Find us where we need to be," we told the Universe. "We ask only one thing—let us both recognize our new home when we see it."

That is what happened. We knew at once. The house and the

land that we found soothed us, nourished us, invited us and welcomed us. Our new home is many things that the cabin is not. It is
open, light, and spacious. It has huge windows and big views.

I thought that the transition from our cabin in the trees would
be difficult, but it wasn't. Fruit drops from the tree when it is
ready. I was ready, and so was Linda. Letting go was easy and natural. I am still in awe of this process. The cabin was perfect for me
when I arrived, and our new home is perfect for me now. Staying
too long, or moving too early, misses the mark. The mark is the
appropriateness that causes the fruit to fall when it is ready.

No wind can bring the fruit down before it is ready to fall, and
when it is ready to fall, nothing can keep it on the branch. Linda
and I flowed with this process into our new home. When I arrived
at our cabin so long ago, I fought it. I decided what I wanted, and
getting it was hard work. Fight or flow, the process has its own
timing, and it creates changes in your life when those changes
need to happen.

PICKING BERRIES

Southern Oregon is blackberry country. They grow everywhere. In the late summer, the berries, which are green at first, and then red, turn deep purple. When that happens, they are juicy and sweet.

Blackberries grow on thorny vines. These vines are hearty plants that grow and spread quickly. Where Linda and I live, they cover fences, stream-sides, and roadsides. As delicious and desirable as blackberries are, there is always more than enough for everyone. In some places, the location of a blackberry patch is a precious secret. In southern Oregon, the secrets are many and known to all. There are so many blackberry patches that, during the season, anyone can pick as many berries as she wants whenever she wants them.

This is the part about berry picking I love the best. No matter how many berries I pick, thousands more mature the next day. For me, picking berries is an experience of the abundance of the Earth, and the abundance of the Universe. What I need is always there.

The thorns on a blackberry plant cover every surface—stems, leaves, and even the bases of the flowers. They all point down the vine in the same direction so that if one catches you (and if one does, many others usually do) you must stop immediately and gently move in the direction that the thorns are growing to release yourself. If you try to pull away, the thorns will not let you go. They dig in deeper and, if you don't stop, they will tear flesh.

Picking berries without getting caught on the thorns, and knowing how to release yourself when you do, is part of a learning experience that has more value than putting berries on the table. How many times have you gotten caught in a circumstance, tried to pull away without taking time to assess your situation, and been injured? Sometimes your circumstances will not release you until you stop, relax, and move with the flow. If you react to your circumstances without thinking, you make things worse. One of my favorite berry patches taught me that, again, one recent morning. I intend to remember the lesson long after the berries in it are gone and the patches around our home have withered for the winter.

Appreciating abundance, awareness, and patience are important lessons. Every experience that you have in the Earth school is designed to help you learn them. Realizing that is appreciating abundance. Taking the time to learn from your experiences is patience. Seeing the abundance around you and the value of your experiences is awareness.

What thorny circumstances in your life are teaching you to appreciate abundance, to be patient, and to become aware?

An Open Heart

THE TENTH NUMBER

Our last event was in Chicago. It was called "A Celebration of Your Soul." This gathering was created almost completely by a team of volunteers in Chicago, who, over several months, became a deeply bonded family.

At the end of the event, which extended through a weekend, I had the honor to sit in a circle with this family while they shared their feelings, appreciation for each other, and awe at what they had created. Their awe was not only at the power and beauty of the event, but also at the power and beauty of the relationship that they had cocreated among them.

One young man, a thoughtful businessman, pondered a long time before he spoke.

"I feel as though my heart has taken the form of a lock that requires ten numbers to open it. Opening my heart is the most important thing to me. I already have the first nine numbers, but I need to get the tenth number from someone else."

"Someone has just given me the tenth number, and my heart is open for the first time. But when it happened, I realized that the tenth number is only good for one moment. I need another tenth number for the next moment, and another for the next."

There were tears in his eyes, and he was laughing at the same time. He had unlocked his heart, and he saw that keeping it unlocked requires other people.

Unlocking your heart is not something that happens once and

is done with. It is a moment-to-moment process that will not stop until you go home—until you die. It requires intention and determination. Those are the first nine numbers. You must provide them. Then it requires someone else. Other people must provide you with the tenth number. They can't do that if you aren't listening to them, or you don't care about what they are saying.

The young man shook his head in wonderment as he spoke. Then he laughed.

He had stepped into the present moment and, for that moment, we had stepped into it with him.

THE HONOR OF ALL

Our Native American brothers and sisters say that the hurt of one is the hurt of all, and the honor of one is the honor of all.

Some people think that this is merely a poetical statement. It is not. It is an accurate observation, not sentimentality or wishful thinking. We all saw this clearly at a recent event in which ninety-two people assembled in the Santa Cruz Mountains to explore and experience authentic power—the alignment of the personality with the soul.

After an exercise, toward the end of the event when laughter and tears began to surface more easily, a big man with the body of an athlete looked at me with wonder on his face and asked to share his experience with the group.

"My partner was my wife," he began. "We decided to do this exercise together, even though we had decided to sit apart throughout the event."

He was silent for a moment, and then he continued. "I could feel in my stomach when my wife was frightened because her stomach became agitated. When it did, my stomach became agitated, too. Then I felt energy move into her chest. It became tight, and my chest became tight, too."

His wife, sitting beside him, nodded her head slightly, in surprise, while her husband described her, and his, experiences.

"Then her throat became tight and, at the same time, my

throat became tight. I knew exactly what she was experiencing because I was experiencing it."

There were tears in his eyes now.

"I also knew when she let go of the fear that she felt. It was a remarkable experience. I felt her crying tears of happiness. That was when I noticed tears running down my cheeks. I felt my face with my hand, and it was wet. I was crying, also."

He moved his head from side to side as though still trying to believe his words.

"I felt my *wife's* tears on *my* face!" he said, amazed.

We were all silent. His wife's tears and his wife's joy were not separate from his own. For a moment, he was not separate from us, either. His wonder was our wonder. His pain was our pain.

What would you do differently if you could feel the pain of others and the joy of others? What does your heart say to you at the thought that you can? What does it say to you at the thought that eventually you will?

Would you be more gentle with others? Would you be more compassionate with yourself? How would you begin the process of living with awareness in a world in which the hurt of one is the hurt of all, and honor of one is the honor of all?

HONG KONG

I was twenty-three. Hong Kong was hot and sticky. I wore my new suit and tie, anyway. I liked the way that I looked in it. I liked being in a hotel. I liked not wearing a uniform. I was a civilian, and I reveled in it.

I was an ex–Special Forces officer—an ex–Green Beret at a time when Green Berets were heroes or villains to almost everyone. The smells of Vietnam were still in my nose. The sounds of helicopters, artillery, low-flying jets, and the grunts of boys carrying more weight than they could bear through mud and jungle were still in my ears. I was one of those boys, but I saw myself as a man. I had worked long and hard to be able to do that. I was also a walking explosive ready to detonate.

I couldn't sleep at night without a weapon close to my bed. I avoided cameras. Anonymity was part of my identify. I was one who led Top Secret patrols on Top Secret missions for Top Secret reasons. I was so unsure of myself that I could not have faced the world without that identity. It was still my identity as I stood on the street in front of my hotel. The uniform, including my beret, was gone, but inside I still wore it. I would wear it for a very long time, taking pride in it, feeling superior because of it, holding myself at a distance because of it.

I took one last drag on my cigarette—the kind that made me feel like a cowboy roping cattle—then I dropped it to the sidewalk and squashed it under my shoe. I always liked doing that. It made me feel that people were watching me in admiration. I felt that way in the jungle, too. It was only now and then, in the jungle, that I realized that no one was watching.

As I started to walk away, I felt a tap on my shoulder.

I turned and, to my surprise, I was greeted by the smiling face of a small old man. He was beaming at me with every wrinkle. His right hand was extended toward me and between his thumb and forefinger he held my cigarette butt—now squashed. His smile was irresistible. I felt good just looking at him.

"Oh!" I said, realizing that he was offering it to me. I held my hand out, palm up. He placed the butt into it, still smiling that wonderful smile. "Thank you," I quickly said and put it into the pants pocket of my new suit. It seemed the natural thing to do, and I felt good doing it.

As I walked away I thought to myself, "My! The people in Hong Kong keep their city clean!"

I didn't think about that incident again for years. When I did, I began to see how exceptional it was. Why hadn't I become offended? Why had I suddenly become warm, sensitive, and appreciative? Where had my macho identity gone?

Twenty-five years after it happened, I realized that I had met a Master that day. The old man modeled to me many things that I would spend the last part of my life striving to create in myself. I felt no judgment from him, or hostility, or anger. He embraced me, a foreigner with a different color skin who had befouled his home. His smile fed me, although at the time I did not even know that I was hungry.

Now I am becoming an old man, too. I still think about him, three decades after he stood before me, smiling, with my cigarette butt in his outstretched hand. He has become very important to me. I ask myself often, "Can I touch people the same way that he touched me? Do I have the goodness of heart, openness of character, and strength of compassion? Will I be able to create these things in myself before I die?"

We were born to touch each other. What does your touch feel like to others? Do you reach out in anger, disdain, or resentment? Do you need to please, or need to push away? Can you do what is appropriate, act with an open heart, and trust the Universe? Do differences of language, clothing, skin color, or behavior determine your thoughts? Can you be who you are in a world where everyone is different? Can you let the world be different and remain who you are?

Sometimes, when I ask myself these questions, I think about my friend in Hong Kong. He has left the Earth school long ago, but he is still a part of me. I don't know his name, but I don't need to. I know enough about him. He shared all that was important in that moment and I am still enriched by what he shared.

What are you sharing, and who is it enriching?

THE YEAR AFTER

In that first year after September 11, 2001, we had much to think about, feel, and picture again and again. A double nightmare of burning jet fuel hundreds of feet above Manhattan, collapsing steel and concrete, and crowds in another part of the world dancing in jubilation at the horror. Stark brutality and cheering people burning American flags combined into a tapestry of pain and shock, celebration and laughter that seem forever impossible to contain in one memory.

In fact, they always come together. September 11, 2001, was a different day only because it allowed us to see both anguish and joy, side by side on television, united by a single event that was devastating to us and gratifying to others. Those who cheered our grief and celebrated our agony could not see us as brothers or sisters, fathers or mothers, grandparents or grandchildren. They saw us as cruel and inhuman and our attackers as brave and just. For a brief moment, their own pain disappeared into the joy of seeing in pain those who inflict pain.

Now it is our turn. We cannot see those who wronged us as brothers or sisters, fathers or mothers, grandparents or grandchildren. We see them as cruel and inhuman and we see ourselves as brave and just. We seek to escape our pain, ever so briefly, by inflicting pain.

First there is revenge and joy for one and suffering and grief for the other. Then there is revenge and joy for the other and suffering and grief for the one. Back and forth these roles change through the days, the weeks, the years, and the centuries. Back and forth they have changed through millennia. Where there is the perception of a brother as inhuman, there is joy in the thought of his pain. There is celebration in her despair.

Soon it will be our turn to celebrate revenge while others grieve—and seek revenge against us. Who is the villain in this picture, and who is the victim? Who is just, and who is not? Who is unjust, and who is not?

The picture remains the same, and has remained the same through human history. Only the costumes of the people in the picture have changed. Sometimes they wear costumes of Christians and Muslims, and sometimes they are dressed as Arabs and Jews. At other times the people in the picture are Chinese, and at yet other times they are European or African. There will always be different costumes in the picture. So long as the picture remains, suffering and grief will coexist with celebration and joy, each feeding upon the other in an ugly frenzy.

There is only one way to change this picture. You must change yourself. You cannot change the perception of a brother or sister as inhuman in someone else. You can only change it in yourself. You cannot challenge the need for revenge in someone else. You can only challenge it in yourself. The work that is required to change the picture requires your courage and your heart. It requires you to see clearly the brutality that pervades the human experience, and to change it in the only place you can change it permanently—in yourself.

Are you enraged? Will you seek revenge, or do you have the

courage to step out of the picture? Are you humiliated? Will you seek to humiliate others, or will you step out of the picture? Are you grieving? Will you cause others to grieve, again?

Can you do these things now, or will you wait for another year after?

YOUR BEST FRIEND

Last January a friend came to spend some time with Linda and me. As she drove toward our home, she encountered a severe snowstorm. The road became impassable, and, although she was only seven miles away, she checked in to a motel.

It was fortunate that she did. It was the last room available and she had to stay there two days and two nights while the storm raged around us.

Our friend is an artist. She also happened to have several boxes of glasses that she had bought for a friend and was in the process of delivering, along with her own paints and brushes that she traveled with. During her stay in the motel, she painted all of the glasses with different designs, scenes, and colors. She became a phenomenon to the other guests. They came by from all of the rooms to see her creations, which soon covered every surface that could support a glass. She made friends with most of them, and most of them made friends with each other.

By the time the storm was over and she could travel the last few miles to our home, she was glowing with the experience.

"It was a wonderful time," she told us, laughing with delight at the memories. "I never thought that being caught in a snowstorm in a small town for so long could be so much fun."

"I am happy that I like people so much," she said with satisfaction.

Then she thought a moment, and said, "If I had to be snow-bound with someone, I am glad it was me."

Can you say that about yourself? Do you like your company? If you had to choose a best friend, would it be you?

The things that you don't like about yourself are the same things that you do not like about other people. The way that you treat yourself is also the way that you treat other people. If you don't like yourself, you will assume that other people don't like you, either, no matter what they say or do. You won't let them come close, even if they want to be your friend. If you think that you are unlovable, you won't be able to imagine that anyone else could think that you are lovable, either.

If you like yourself, you will like other people. If you enjoy your company, you won't feel intruded upon by the company of others. How you feel about yourself is more than a private internal matter. It determines how you are with others, and, ultimately, how you are with the Universe.

It you do not like yourself, you will not like the Universe. If you are your best friend, the Universe will be your best friend, also.

Can you imagine that?

I KNEW YOU'D COME

A friend told me a story that his minister told him: Two young men who grew up as best friends enlisted in the Marines and were sent to Vietnam. They were caught in a firefight and one of them was mortally wounded in a clearing. With the North Vietnamese on one side of the clearing and the Marines on the other, the wounded man called again and again to his friend.

The sergeant in charge of the patrol shouted, "Don't think about going. He's not going to live and you'll die, too, if you try to help him."

Breaking away from the sergeant, the young man ran into the clearing, under fire, and dragged his friend back. By that time, his friend was dead.

"I told you so!" yelled the sergeant.

"When I got there he was alive," said the young man, "and he said, 'I knew you'd come.'"

I do not know if this story actually happened the way I was told, but from the perspective of the soul, it is true. Each of us has contracts with the Universe that we accept before we enter the Earth school. These are sacred contracts. They do not predetermine our experiences. Nothing can do that because no one, not even nonphysical Teachers, know what decisions we will make as we encounter the circumstances of our lives.

Souls agree to provide one another opportunities, in certain circumstances that might occur in the Earth school, to learn the lessons that each incarnates to learn and to give the gifts that each was born to give. They do not know how their personalities will choose to respond, but they agree to provide the opportunities to make choices.

That is how many individuals come into your life—they are souls with whom you have made agreements prior to your birth. Have you thought about that possibility before? Even individuals whom you consider your enemies, and those whom you judge harshly, are friends from the perspective of your soul. They agreed to meet you, under certain conditions, and you agreed to meet them, under certain conditions. Your choices continually create conditions and as they do, souls appear to keep their agreements.

No one you meet in the Earth school is a stranger, and all are your friends. From the perspective of your soul, you are friends or you would not be together at all. You can experiment with seeing the way your soul sees by inwardly greeting each person in your life, whether ally or foe, as the young Marine greeted his dear friend. "I knew you'd come."

Developing Awareness

HORSE STANCE

When I was on Taiwan for a year I decided to learn a form of the martial art kung fu. I saw it everywhere in the movies that played in almost every theater on the island. Fighters using kung fu twirled, kicked, jumped, and punched with grace and skill through every life-threatening challenge, including dragons, sorcerers, assassins, and armies. So advanced were their skills that they could see in the dark and moved so quickly they were all but invisible. I didn't expect to become magical, but I wanted to learn a form of hand-to-hand combat beyond the crude moves the Army had taught me. I was in excellent physical condition and my self-image as an ex–Green Beret and a manly, formidable warrior, along with the kung fu movies, combined to excite me when I met a man whom I discovered taught kung fu.

I asked him to teach me, and he agreed. On my first day, he arranged my feet in an awkward position. "This is the Horse Stance," he said. Then he told me to stand that way without moving, and walked away. Soon my legs, especially the quadriceps muscles in my thighs, began to ache. By the time he returned, my legs were quivering with the strain. He gave me a gentle push on my right shoulder and I almost fell over! He rearranged my feet slightly and walked away again. I remained that way until the end of the lesson.

My next lesson, and the next and the next, were the same. I stood in the same position, and he watched, sometimes pushed me gently, made a small adjustment, and left. My legs began to grow accustomed to this strange and painful position, but the process was slow and they never stopped hurting.

By the second month, I was becoming impatient. I wanted to twirl, kick, jump, and punch. I wanted to move in the fluid, lethal, villain-killing ways I saw in the movies. Instead, I was standing day after day, not moving at all, and feeling the pain in my legs.

"How long do I have to do this?" I complained. "As long as necessary," he said, and left again.

The experience of learning kung fu was not what I thought it would be. My impatience grew into exasperation, even as my legs began to strengthen and the pain in them began to lessen. At last, I asked my teacher, "How long did *you* have to do this when you learned kung fu?"

"Three years," he answered calmly, adjusted my shoulders slightly, and walked away again.

His answer shocked me. It was not because of the enormous amount of time involved (from my perspective), but also because at that moment I realized that kung fu, and perhaps all the martial arts, were very different from what I had imagined. I imagined that I would be able to learn kung fu and remain the same person. Now I realized that learning kung fu was going to *change me*. I could learn kung fu, but the person who acquired the ability was going to be different from the person who set about to learn it.

I left Taiwan long before I was able to learn kung fu in anything like the way I had wildly imagined. But I did learn how to stand firmly on the Earth, anchored like a tree, strong like a horse. I had begun to build a foundation—the Horse Stance. My teacher was wise enough not to waste his time or mine teaching me movements before I knew how to stand while doing them. He would not let me believe I was learning kung fu in that way, because he knew that nothing he taught me without the Horse Stance would benefit me as it would when I had developed the foundation that practicing kung fu requires.

Spiritual growth is like that, too. You must first build a foundation. You may want to spring into a new life of kindness and compassion, a life that is grounded and appropriate in every way, but until you build the foundation to support such a life, you will not be able to accomplish it. Emotional awareness is one of the foundations of authentic power—the alignment of your personality with your soul. It requires commitment and courage. It is painful to become emotionally aware because there is so much pain in the world, and that pain is in you. There is also joy in the world, but you cannot reach it until you can reach the pain you feel, also. Then you can begin to cultivate the sources of your joy and challenge the causes of your pain. That is how you create authentic power.

Your emotional health and your spiritual development cannot be separated. You cannot be angry, resentful, jealous, and live in violent fantasies and negative judgments and be compassionate and kind at the same time. Kindness and compassion are the skills you need to develop. Awareness of your emotions is your Horse Stance.

Don't forget to build your foundation.

SENSATIONAL

Recently Linda and I returned to Maui. Each of the Hawaiian islands has its own feel, even though all of them are Hawaiian. They are all beautiful. Maui has a deep, healing, gentle feel to me. No matter how often we return, I feel this gentle, healing energy. I first came in 1990 on a book tour for *The Seat of the Soul*. Some of the people I met then became friends and they have received me, and later, Linda and me, as family. In Hawaiian, family is called *ohana*. So Linda and I have had *ohana* on Maui for a long time and we visit each other and welcome each other whenever we can.

One of the members of our *ohana* guides people to remote parts of Maui—to waterfalls, bamboo forests, hidden beaches, rugged cliffs, and special places in the history and tradition of the island. Each time I think that I have visited them all, I learn there are dozens I have yet to see. The waterfall that Linda and I hiked to one morning was one of those. The trail crisscrosses a stream that begins high in the mountains above the valley we were climbing. It follows the stream through bamboo thickets and verdant growths of fern and trees, bringing us to the stream again and again. Each time we found a perfect set of stones to step across. From the mouth of the valley to the waterfall, and probably beyond to the forests above, low stone walls filled the valley. They were built by ancient Hawaiian farmers to grow tarot. These farmers were the best tarot farmers in the world. They knew how to water one terraced field after another with the stream, and then to release its water, crystal clear, into the ocean at the mouth of the valley.

We heard the waterfall before we could see it. It was hidden in a rock cove. We had to enter the cove directly, stepping carefully along a ledge before we could round the massive stone outcropping that hid it. It fell from the stream above about twenty feet into a small pool, filling the rock-enclosed area around the small pool with the pounding sounds of water on water. Rock walls rose on three sides of us. Even if there were sunshine, which there was not on that cloudy day, none would have found its way into this grotto.

Linda and I tested the water. It was cold and refreshing. We liked that it was refreshing, but we were hesitant because it was cold. I took off my sandals and put my feet into the small pool. It was wonderful. Linda did the same. We looked at each other with the same question: Shall we jump in? There would be no sun to warm us when we got out, but we had hiked over an hour and the pool and the waterfall promised the kind of refreshment that comes only from clear, clean, cold water on a hot day.

I decided to experiment. Instead of bracing against the cold, I wondered what sensations I would feel if I dived into the pool. I stopped thinking in terms of labels, such as *cold* and *chilling*, and started to think in terms of *sensations*. I became curious about the sensations the pool would create in me. I took a few steps into the pool, up to my knees, and dived forward. My body was filled with sensations. They were thrilling. They woke me from the slumber of the long, hot hike. They filled me with electricity. I was alert and present from my toes to the crown of my head. The sound of the waterfall filled my ears, and my body tingled as though it were alive. It was.

That was my lesson about sensations and how different sensations are from the labels of sensations. Labels are thoughts that occur in your mind. Sensations happen in your body. Some thoughts are frightening and some thoughts are inviting. Sensations are sensations. I do not like cold water, but I liked the sensations that filled my body. I do not like to be chilled, but I liked the refreshing sensations that filled me. Perhaps if I had thought about it, I would have decided—or experienced—that I was cold, and then chilled. But I was neither. I was filled with sensations.

See if you can find the difference between labels and sensations in your life. Can you recognize when you are bracing against a label instead of opening to sensations? When you can, experiment with diving into your sensations directly. You may find you have left your labels behind.

WAVES

I was happy when a Hawaiian friend invited Linda and me to paddle an outrigger canoe. The ancient Hawaiians traveled thousands of miles in these small craft, which, in the old days, were made from the trunk of a koa tree. Master builders searched for the perfect tree, prayed, and performed ceremonies asking for permission from the tree to use it, and then a ring of ocean salt was put around the base of the tree to help it make the transition from a tree into a seagoing vessel. Finally, the entire community pulled the tree down the mountain to the distant ocean, where it was transformed into a sleek seven-person vessel. Because the hull was narrow and, therefore, unstable, a pontoon was strapped onto it with two struts—the outrigging. In these simple craft, the Hawaiians traveled their oceans by celestial navigation.

Now it was time for Linda and me to paddle. Our canoe was a sleek and beautiful modern version made of fiberglass. Our friend, a very strong man, welcomed us warmly and immediately put us at ease. I asked him what it is like to row on the open water in such a small craft with so few companions.

"Each journey is a relationship with the ocean," he said. "We listen to the waves. Some of the waves are quite large. They say to us, 'This way, my relatives. Ride my back. I will take you with me to my brother who is waiting for you. Behind him is my sister. See? She is waving at you! She is saying, "Come to me, my relatives! I will take you with me." '

"Each wave is different, so we listen carefully to them and we move as they guide us," he continued, making a snaking motion with his hand to indicate the ever-changing path from one wave to another—from one brother to another to a sister, from relative to relative. In that moment, I realized that my friend and his companions do not conquer the ocean when they travel successfully on it. They journey with family, going where their relatives take them.

Can you journey through your life in the same way? Do you see difficulties as obstacles, or as experiences that show you where to go, how to change your course so you will reach your goal? Can you think of your experiences as our friend thinks of waves—as relatives that help you on your journey to authentic power—the alignment of your personality with your soul?

Your destination is a life of meaning, fulfillment, creativity, and joy—a life free of your fears, obsessions, compulsions, and addictions, without the insecurities that others activate so easily and the torments they create in you. When you resist your experiences, you ignore the guidance they offer. Your anger, resentment, jealousy, and fear each show you, in their own way, what you need to change in yourself to reach your destination. "Come," they say. "Listen to me."

Are you listening?

FATHER AND DAUGHTER

Even when you think you know your intention, you may have other intentions that you are not aware of and, if so, they will shape your experiences. Unconscious intentions are hidden agendas. If you don't know you have one, you will be surprised by what it creates.

At one of our events a young woman excitedly raised her hand. "I have been in therapy with my father for two years," she began, "and it is going slowly. He is a difficult man and sometimes I have wondered why I continue. Now I realize," she said with surprise, "that I have been in therapy with him because I wanted him to change so I could love him! Now I can hardly wait to get back to therapy so I can love him the way he is!" This insight transformed her intention to control her father into a loving acceptance of him as he was. I don't know whether or not it affected her father, but I could see how deeply it affected her.

When you are aware of your intentions, you are no longer surprised by the consequences they create. The young woman at last understood, and so did we, why progress with her father had been slow.

An intention is your reason, or motivation, for acting. It is the consciousness behind your action. The young woman thought she intended to heal her relationship with her father, but actually she intended to change him. How do you feel when someone tries to change you? Do you resent it? I suspect her father felt similarly. How do you feel when someone accepts you? I suspect her father felt similarly about that, too.

Searching for your hidden agendas is worth the effort. Before you speak, or act, ask yourself, "What is my intention?" and then listen for an answer. Sooner or later you will hear one. Then you can decide to keep your intention or change it. In other words, you can choose the experience you will create consciously.

THE STREETS OF LOS ANGELES

A friend once told me of her fear of the streets of Los Angeles
after seeing television reports of violence in the southern part
of that city. "More police," she thought, "and more prosecutors
are needed. "The trouble," she stated with authority, "is lack of
parental discipline, too many illegal drugs, and moral decay. We
need stern authority in this matter," she concluded, "to make our
streets safe once again."

Several nights later she dreamed of her first teen romance. She
was attracted to a young man named Thom. Thom returned her
affection, and in an innocent way a romance developed between
them. Then, without reason, Thom became distant. His coldness
grew and, at last, when they passed in the hall he would not even
look at her.

She was crushed. Then she became angry. She glared at Thom
when she saw him. Her thoughts filled with fantasies of revenge,
of Thom hurting as much as she hurt. The more she hurt, the
more frequent and violent her fantasies became. Years later,
when they were both out of school, Thom gained the courage to
tell her that he had become frightened of his attraction to her.
The stronger his attraction became, the more frightened he became. He built a wall between them because of his attraction to
her. Then her angry thoughts and violent fantasies humiliated
her. She realized that she had accused Thom in her mind of be-

trayal, and had attempted to punish him in her mind. The dream brought all of this back to her.

"Why," she asked herself, "did I have this dream now?" The answer jolted her as much as the dream. "I realized," she said, "that there is a very close connection between what happens in my mind and what happens in my life that I never saw before. I always judged violence on the streets as though it had nothing to do with me. I think now that it does. I commit the same violence! For all those years, Thom was not safe on the streets of my mind."

The streets of her mind and the streets of Los Angeles had ceased to be different for her. She saw violence on one—the Los Angeles streets—as a reflection of violence on the other—the streets in her mind.

Can you make the same connection? Can you find in yourself, at this moment, the same violence that you fear or disdain in other people and other places? If you can, you will not judge others so harshly, even those who are violent. You will also begin the process of creating a world without violence, or at least with less violence.

Until then, you will contribute to the violence in the world, not reduce it.

Life Lessons

BEYOND MOTHER-DAUGHTER

Our retreats continue to become more profound for me each year. We begin them by doing our best to invoke a sacred space. Then we introduce the basics of spiritual partnership—for everyone, not just couples—and then we spend some time in a circle practicing them. That is when things get deep and difficult. It is when differences arise and communication either stays shallow and in the head or goes deep into the heart. I wait for this to happen, and, so far, it always has.

Midway through the most difficult part of our retreat, a woman shared her frustration and resentment over needing to care for her elderly mother in the advanced stages of Alzheimer's disease—a mother with whom she had a distant relationship all of her life.

"You don't know what it is like to be with her," she exclaimed. "One day she thinks I am *her* mother. Other times she thinks I am her sister. I usually go along with her, but the last time, I decided not to."

"Do you know who I am?" I asked her.

"You are my mother," she replied.

"No," I said, "I am not your mother."

"You are my sister," she tried again.

"No, I am not your sister."

The woman began to cry softly as she continued.

"Then my mother looked directly at me and said, 'I don't

know if you're my mother. I don't know if you're my sister. I only know that my soul needs to be with you!' "

No one in the circle spoke a word.

"My mother is not a religious person, or a metaphysical person," said the woman. "It was her soul talking to my soul. I knew it and I could feel it."

Since then the experience of mother and daughter changed dramatically for the daughter. Instead of resenting her mother, she looks at her as the source of her deepest lesson about Life, and the bonds that connect us.

Those bonds exist moment to moment, whether we are aware of them or not. When we become aware of them, our lives change. Resentment turns to gratitude, anger becomes compassion, and the perception of senselessness becomes the experience of meaning.

Awareness of the bonds that connect us is multisensory perception. Appreciating them is reverence. Striving to behave accordingly is the pursuit of authentic power.

HEARING AND LISTENING

The woman in the second row rose to speak.

"My daughter had an accident when she was an infant. When I learned that she was deaf, it changed my life. Since that time, I devoted myself to supporting her in every way that I could. We sent her to special schools and went to schools ourselves.

"Last year, when she graduated from high school, my fears arose again. I was worried about what her life would be like in college. I again began looking for ways to support her. But a few weeks later, she came to me.

"Taking my hands, she said, 'Mom, you're messing me up. I want you to learn to hear the way I do.' "

I was deeply touched, and I think everyone in the retreat was, too. The daughter did not think of herself as disadvantaged. On the contrary, she did not like being shaped into her mother's image of her as a disadvantaged person. More than that, she had gifts to give to her mother (and to others) that she was longing to share.

Every life in the Earth school is perfect, including your own, even if it is not the way that you think it ought to be. The daughter could have chosen to believe her loving mother, and pitied herself the way that her mother pitied her. She didn't. She chose to live her life and to share the beauty of it.

What choices are you making about your life? Are you listening to what your life is telling you, or to what others are telling you about your life? The mother thought that her daughter couldn't hear and she was worried about that. Her daughter wasn't worried. She wanted to be heard in her own way. Who was deaf? The daughter, or the mother?

When the mother finally listened to her beloved daughter, she began to hear, too.

FIERCE GRACE

Six years ago, one of the pioneers of the "New Age" suffered a stroke. His name is Ram Dass. I first heard him speak several years before his stroke. He was articulate and active in his presentation, joking with us, telling stories, and even leading us in a song. The stroke paralyzed one side of his body, leaving a leg and arm immobile. It also left him with a slow manner of speaking, resulting from the necessity for him to search for words and concepts to clothe his meaning, something like looking in a closet for the right clothing, but not remembering where it is hanging.

Ram Dass adopted the Hindu tradition, or rather, it adopted him. His early books brought Hindu philosophy and perceptions to millions of flower children. Now he is in his seventies and a wheelchair. "When people saw me after the stroke, they would say, 'poor Ram Dass,' but I was not so quick to agree.

"I lived a graced life, but then came this stroke," he told us, pointing to his paralyzed side with his mobile hand. "How could I reconcile my grace with this stroke? Doing that took a long time. Then it began to occur to me that my stroke was fierce grace."

His words came slowly, but each one hit the mark. Listening to him was like watching arrows shot one at a time, slowly, and each one precisely penetrating the center of a target. "Before I had my stroke, I received tiny pieces of grace. When I drove to the store, for example, I visualized a parking place waiting for me and someone would pull out of the spot I needed as I arrived," he said with twinkling eyes. "Now I have a blue placard in my car and there are parking places waiting for me *everywhere!*" We all laughed as it became apparent that his slow delivery did not obstruct his humor.

"When I spoke to audiences before my stroke, there were always a few people with crossed legs and arms, looking at their watches," Ram Dass explained. "I tried, but I couldn't reach their hearts. Now this wheelchair is doing it!" He laughed at his own words, slapping his mobile arm on his knee in glee. "I have to speak very slowly now," he continued, ". . . and that gives you more time to think." He was exactly right. We hung on each word to see how Ram Dass would finish his sentence. By the time he finished it, his first words had time to sink in deeply.

"Before my stroke, I saw myself as a spiritual being in a body. I looked at my body as a vehicle for my spiritual growth but not important in itself. The stroke taught me that my body is important." Last he told us of his travels to healers, and of his experience with the suffering and faith of those he had met because of his stroke. "Most important," he concluded, "I realized that over the many years I have been a spiritual teacher, I had lost the tender love that I got from my guru. Now I have it back."

He concluded by answering questions from the large audience, each answer bringing us laughter and insight. He told us of his plans to live where people could come to his retreats instead of his traveling to be with them, because, he explained, "this wheelchair won't fit into airplane johns!"

I left the event deeply touched by the depth of meaning and purpose in the life of Ram Dass, as I thought about the life he would have created if he had agreed with those who declared, "poor Ram Dass." I thought about his humor and wisdom, and the gifts he had given to himself and to me. I wondered whether I would have the courage to apply my wisdom to my life if I were in his position. I wondered what circumstances in my life I was complaining about instead of receiving gifts from. I am still looking for them. I do not want to ignore the grace that comes into my life, even when it is fierce. Especially when it is fierce.

What in your life is tormenting you? What circumstance are you resisting? What situations are you regretting? Do you say things like, "If only this had not happened? If only I had not . . ." Examine your life closely. It may take you a long time, the way it took Ram Dass a long time, to see the grace in your difficult experiences, and to use that grace to transform and enrich your life, but Ram Dass showed us that it is worth the effort.

Can you use your experiences to grow spiritually as well as Ram Dass used his?

THE URGENT AND THE IMPORTANT

We were striving yet again to restructure our small organization into greater effectiveness and efficiency and, at the same time, into alignment with the intentions of the soul—harmony, cooperation, sharing, and reverence for Life. Our old model, in which everyone approved everything before anything happened, had broken down. We knew that we didn't want the command and control type of structure that most businesses and nonprofit organizations use. We didn't yet have a new model.

As we sat in a circle deliberating, an urbane man with corporate experience at senior levels spoke.

"We must distinguish between what is urgent and what is important," he said matter-of-factly. "We could accomplish all of the urgent things that we desire without accomplishing anything that is important."

He had articulated our challenge exactly—how to do the urgent things that need to be done without losing ourselves in them.

"What is important," he continued, "is bringing the patterns that run us to the light of consciousness."

Staying on time is an urgent matter. Remaining aware of what you are feeling while you meet your timelines is important. Catching an airplane is urgent. Remembering that your taxi driver is a soul like yourself is important. Competition is urgent. Cooperation, sharing, harmony, and reverence for Life are important.

How much of your attention is focused on the urgent, and how much is focused on the important?

LOYALTY

As we approached the cemetery, I could see a flagpole directly ahead, as though the street were an instrument designed to align our vision with the flag. The flag was at half-mast. Not until later did I realize that it flew in honor of my father.

As we drove through the gates, they closed behind us. This was my father's chosen resting place for his ashes—a small national cemetery in the heart of the Midwest. He had not asked for military honors, although he gave up his career and left his young family, including me, to defend his country. For three years he lived and fought in the South Pacific against the Japanese army. It was those years of his life that qualified him to choose this small, quiet, immaculate cemetery as the place my mother, my sister, Linda, and I would gather to put his ashes into the Earth.

We asked the staff, small-town Midwesterners like my father had been for five decades, if we might be alone. They politely left us to our thoughts and each other. The cemetery had a peaceful, respectful feeling to me. The old stone walls, the clean rows of white marble markers, each honoring a son or a daughter and each thanking a veteran, calmed me. The presence of a great country—my own—was palpable to me, and the deep and dramatic struggles that took the lives of so many as it, like every other human collective, defended or extended its values and perceptions with blood.

My country was honoring my father for his loyalty. Congressional funds kept this small piece of history and the present green and orderly. Like a Zen garden, it soothed my mind and put me at ease. Soldiers from wars past and their relatives surrounded us. Lives filled with challenges and struggles that were completed, or not, a century ago stood with us.

I placed the small urn into the small hole in the Earth. The soil was brown and rich. Each of us took a turn speaking—to each other and to Dad. Linda watched, holding my mother's hand. We were silent for a while, and then we started slowly back. I stopped, turned, and without thinking did something I could not have anticipated. I saluted my father. We were both Army officers in our youth, but he was the senior. That salute—my first in thirty years—felt deeply good. My ceremony was complete, but my experience of the cemetery, and my salute, have stayed with me.

My father was true, honest, highly principled, and trustworthy. Those were words he chose to describe himself, and they were accurate. I learned loyalty from him, and integrity. As the gates opened once again to the public and we left the cemetery, I pondered the depth and power of loyalty—the ability to serve and support a cause greater than oneself.

While humanity was limited in its perceptions to the five senses, that greater cause to most individuals was a family, clan, tribe, community, or nation. For others it was a belief, or an idea. Now that we are becoming multisensory—expanding beyond the limitations of the five senses—that greater cause is becoming Life. Life that includes all living things, all things that do not appear to be living, all thoughts, all actions, all customs, all beliefs, and all colors. This is the only loyalty that now joins. All others divide. Loyalty to Life brings together cultures, nations, tribes, races, and religions. It is the only idea that springs from the heart, not from the mind. It is the medicine for our illness, food for our hunger, and drink for our thirst.

The loyalty for which my father was honored is the same loyalty that now fills millions of humans who are becoming aware of themselves as threads in a larger fabric of Life, and moving with deep dedication to contribute all that they are to it. It is the natural expression of the goodness of human nature, flowing toward all that it can bless, and all that can bless it. It is the only loyalty, so long in coming, that can harm none and benefits all.

It is the loyalty that you were born to give, and to receive.

SMALL BROWN SEDAN

Your internal experiences tell you important things about yourself. I learned how important those things can be one afternoon outside the baggage claim area of an airport while waiting for my ride into a city. That is where this story ended, but it began many years ago at the Chicago airport on the way to my first interview with Oprah Winfrey. To my surprise, a large, shining, black limousine was waiting for me and Linda.

I was excited because I had never ridden in a limousine and embarrassed at the same time because no one I knew had enough money to even think of such a thing. On our next trip to Chicago, another large, black, shining limousine was waiting for us, and on the next trip and the next until I began to expect one each time we arrived. Then, as we began traveling to other cities, shining black limousines were waiting for us there, too, and so I began to expect them at every airport.

At last we came to the airport where this story ends. As I emerged from baggage claim looking for my large, shining, black limousine, I found instead a small, old, brown sedan waiting for me. "How can we get our baggage into that?" I complained. And, "Now Linda and I won't have any privacy for the ride into the city." Really, though, I was angry because I wanted an impressive car to pick me up and a very ordinary car was waiting instead.

As I stood on the sidewalk fuming, I suddenly saw myself from the outside, as someone else would see me, and I was shocked.

Mahatma Gandhi is one of my role models, and he had almost no possessions—only a begging bowl, eyeglasses, and around his waist a piece of clothing that he wove himself. I was not behaving like my image of Gandhi! And I was deeply embarrassed. The pain I felt when the shining, black limousine was not there to greet me showed me a part of myself that I did not know about, but that I very much needed to know about.

If Linda, or anyone else had said, "Gary, you need to know that you are acting very arrogantly," I would have been offended. But I was behaving arrogantly, and my painful internal experiences were drawing my attention to it. Now I am grateful for those painful experiences and that small brown sedan. I think about them often, and what I learned. Each time, I say "Thank you!" with all my heart.

Do you have some painful experiences to thank?

LEAVES

My first visit to a Zen monastery still inspires me. I went to have a Sanskrit reference translated for *The Dancing Wu Li Masters: An Overview of the New Physics,* which I was writing at the time. A monk informed me I would be received by the abbot himself. He led me to large courtyard surrounded by a building that was falling into disrepair. Its once gracious gardens and paths were covered with years of fallen leaves.

"While you are waiting," said the monk, handing me a broom, "please sweep the leaves from the courtyard." I had nothing else to do, so I looked at the huge courtyard, the broom in my hand, and began to sweep. By the time he returned, I had swept fifty feet of walk. The order I had imposed on the otherwise unkempt area pleased me. To my surprise, I regretted handing him back the broom and going to see the abbot.

It seemed to me that I had just begun and I did not want to lose the contentment I felt while I was sweeping the path. I looked back at the path one last time, and as I did a soft breeze blew a leaf onto it, and then two more. My work was being undone before my eyes, but the satisfaction it gave me was mine to keep. I still have it and I remember it when I feel that I have too many important things to do.

Have you spent quality time sweeping lately?

OLD BUFFALOS

My adopted Sioux uncle enjoys telling me stories about animals, but his stories are always more than that. They are also about what we can learn from them to become better humans. One of my favorite stories is about buffalo. The Sioux are high prairie people whose lives revolved around the migrations of great herds of buffalo. Many of the buffalo had been killed, and the Sioux had been forced onto reservations before my uncle, who is in his eighties, was born, but intimate knowledge and relationship with the animals around them were a part of his life as a young boy, just as they are today.

"Do you know, Nephew," he once told me, speaking about buffalo, "that the young are always at the center of the herd where they are protected. The old buffalos move to the outside of the herd so they can offer themselves to their brothers, the wolves, and keep the young safe."

He thought for a moment, then looked at me and said, "I am becoming just like those old buffalos—my life is all for the people now." When my uncle talks about the people, he talks about everyone—black, white, red, yellow, and brown.

He first told me that story ten years ago, and since then it has been one of my favorites. It calls to something in me that is noble enough to think in terms of the well-being of all life, and not just a part of it. Perhaps we are all old buffalos in training.

A WAY OUT OF HELL

An uneasy peace between Muslims and Hindus in India had disintegrated into hatred and violence and the entire state was enflamed with rioting and warfare. In response, Gandhi, a Hindu, announced to the nation that he would not eat again until all violence came to an end. The violence diminished, but Gandhi still refused to eat until it stopped completely, and he became weaker and weaker.

One night as he lay in bed surrounded by worried friends, a wild-eyed Hindu man broke into the room. He threw a piece of food at Gandhi and yelled, "Eat! I am going to hell anyway! I won't have your death on my hands, too!"

Friends rose in alarm, but Gandhi waved them away. "Tell me why you are going to hell," Gandhi said to the man. "I have killed a Muslim boy," the man sobbed. "I swung him by his feet and crushed his head against a wall. Nothing can help me!" No one spoke.

"I know a way out of hell," said Gandhi quietly. The man raised his eyes in disbelief. "Find a young boy," continued Gandhi, "whose parents have been killed and raise him as your own. But raise him as a Muslim."

Gandhi's fast succeeded in stopping the violence throughout India. The quiet did not last, but that vicious and violent period ended temporarily. I do not know what happened to the wild-eyed man, but I think of him often. I think of his anguish, his despair, and his horror at what he had done. I also think about the possibility of his journey out of hell.

The journey Gandhi described requires giving to, caring for, and loving what is most difficult to give to, care for, or love—your hated enemy. Do you have someone in your life you hate too much to ever love? Perhaps it is an abuser, or a Nazi, or one of the young men who destroyed the Twin Towers. Maybe you don't hate anyone that much, but you dislike someone enough to complain about her to your friends. Whether you hate or dislike, you are living in a hell. You do not have to die to experience it. You are in it each time you feel your hatred or dislike. If you don't like the way your hell feels, remember Gandhi and the wild-eyed man, and then see if you can find a way of your own out of hell.

Learning Compassion

COMPASSION AND COURAGE

What does it mean to be compassionate when unrestrained anger and hatred have suddenly, violently taken the lives of thousands of people?

To be compassionate requires that you share your passion with others. The passion of others now is one of pain, of shock, of grieving, and of loss. Compassion allows you to feel those difficult emotions and the pain that lies beneath them. Rage and the need for revenge are the ways that many people will cover the experience of these painful emotions. It is easier to become enraged and to seek revenge, or swear that you will, than it is to experience the pain of loss, the depth of the loss, the grieving, and the fear that is now occurring. When there is unwillingness to experience the depth of these painful emotions, there is a compulsive quality to the anger and to the behaviors that prevent the experience of them. Rage and thoughts of revenge become magnetically attractive not because villains deserve to be punished, but because you are not willing to experience the intensity of the pain that is in you.

The compassionate action in such a circumstance is to experience what you are feeling—to experience the pain and the depth of it in you and then to begin to plan your action from there. Once emotional pain is experienced in that degree—with awareness—your desire will not be to inflict the same pain on others but to avoid that happening again to any individual on the

Earth. That is when and how your creativity will come into focus. If you do not experience your emotions and the depth of the pain that is now within you, you will find yourself irresistibly and self-righteously drawn to thoughts of revenge.

The most compassionate act that you can now choose is also the one that requires the most courage—to feel what you are feeling, to feel beneath the rage and beneath the desire for revenge, if necessary, because there lies pain and it is deep. When you have the courage to feel that pain at the intensity that it is now moving through millions of individuals, then you will begin to see what is necessary to begin to create a world in which this type of pain is not generated.

Therefore, the first step in the creation of compassion is to be compassionate with yourself. Allow yourself to feel all that you are feeling. If you are feeling hatred, do not hate yourself for hating. Compassionate allowance for your human response to tragedy allows you to regain your balance more quickly. Feeling hate does not mean acting on it. It means taking the first step in allowing yourself to become conscious of everything that you are feeling so that you can expand your consciousness to the fear and pain that lie beneath the impulses to hate and to seek revenge.

Do you have the courage to do that? Are you strong enough to feel hatred and not act on it? Are you brave enough to face and feel the pain of loss, of grief, of the horror and the fear that is now pervasive upon our Earth?

Compassion is not for cowards.

COMPASSION AND KARMA

What you sow, you reap. What a collective sows, the collective reaps. What the human family sows, the human family reaps. These overlapping dynamics combine to form the experience of individuals, collectives of individuals, and the human experience. Within these dynamics, individuals, collectives, and humanity encounter the consequences of choices that they have made and are offered opportunities to choose again. With each choice, more consequences are created and more opportunities to choose again present themselves. In the years since the attacks on the World Trade Center and the Pentagon, the consequences of the choices we made in response have become visible. The brutality of the attacks shocked millions and gratified millions. Around the world, individuals who were able to feel the pain of others grieved. Those who could not watched numbly or celebrated the humbling of an evil people. Those who could feel the suffering of others cried for them. Those who could not rejoiced in the pain of villains. This is an ancient pattern. It has repeated itself countless times and the sum of these experiences is the chronicle of human history—brutalities imposed upon humans by humans.

The individuals who attacked us could not grasp our humanity—the humanity of those they attacked. They could not step into the horror of a family suddenly without a father or a mother, a loved one gone without good-bye, or terrible thoughts of those who were dearest in terror and pain. They saw instead inhuman, unholy infidels, blasphemers of the Holy, scourges of the Earth, and enemies of Good. They struck mercilessly because they believed themselves to be superior, to be right, to be good, and to be warriors with the Divine on their side.

They celebrated because, at last, revenge was theirs. They rejoiced because, at last, the pain of others was great. They laughed because, at last, the humiliation of others was deep. They danced because, in their powerlessness, they found a brief moment of relief, of bringing righteousness to the unrighteous, of imposing themselves.

They could not feel the pain they created, but we did, and so did many others around the world. In the tender weeks following the attacks, Americans opened to each other and the world opened to America. Deep bonds of mutual suffering replaced impoliteness, competition, and animosity. The impact of so many souls suddenly gone from the Earth, and the malicious intention behind their deaths, made us vulnerable. Our arrogance disappeared. That was our moment of hope. That was our opportunity to change the course of American history, international relations, and human evolution. It was the opportunity to see our brief collective experience of grief and loss—of the consequences of brutality—as another wave in the ocean of grief and loss that has washed over millions upon millions of humans, including those who struck us without mercy.

This tender moment was our opportunity to return compassion for violence, kindness for brutality, and humanity for inhumanity. It called to us in our pain and our horror. It said to each of us, in the intimacy of our inner lives, "This is what revenge feels like to those who receive it. This is what cruelty feels like to those who experience it. *Do not inflict these terrible experiences upon others. Do not participate in the evolution of violence. Create another path through history. Do you have the courage?"*

If we had heard that call, the consequences that we are now encountering would have been very different. If we had the courage to feel our pain, our humiliation, and the agony of our losses, we would not have been able to create those same experiences in others. Instead, we saw ourselves as victims. We sought revenge. We imposed ourselves self-righteously upon the unrighteous. We perceived ourselves as right, as good, and as warriors with the Divine on our side and, in the process, we created more families without husbands and wives, more loved ones gone without good-byes, and more terrible thoughts of those who were dearest in terror and pain. We became like those who attacked us.

The tender moment after the attacks is gone, but another tender moment can be created. It can be created in you by you. It requires the courage to feel your pain instead of hiding it from yourself with rage, to feel your humiliation without concealing it from yourself with self-righteousness, and your humanity. It requires that you see with compassion even those who have no compassion, because if you have no compassion for those who have no compassion, you become one of them.

In the lengthening aftermath of the attacks on the World Trade Center and the Pentagon, the compassion that millions in every nation felt for the United States has turned into condemnation. Bitter judgments have replaced open hearts and the experience of our common humanity. At this moment, is your heart still open? Can you still feel the pain of others? Do you care about the pain of others? What do you feel? What do you care about? What do you want to create next?

Now is the time to create the tender moment again. Now is always and forever the time to create it, to live in it, and to act in it.

DANGER

In 1959 the Chinese army invaded Tibet, a small country in the Himalayan mountains just north of India, and has brutally occupied it ever since. Mount Everest, the highest mountain on the Earth, is a part of the Himalayan range. Tibet is strikingly beautiful and remote, and in that remote mountain country a special kind of Buddhism took root and bloomed. Virtually the entire country embraced it. Monasteries abounded and meditation, visualizations, and prayer were a deep part of the Tibetan culture. It is possible that the Tibetan culture was the most reverent, nonviolent, and joyful in the world.

You may have seen some of the movies that have been made about Tibet and the Dalai Lama, who is the leader of one of the sects of Tibetan Buddhism and also the leader of his country. He has been in exile in India since shortly after the Chinese invasion. The Chinese have methodically and relentlessly destroyed all that they can of the Tibetan culture and are replacing it with their own. The temples have been desecrated or defiled, valuable art has been shipped to China, and teachers and monks have been killed. Tens of thousands of Tibetans now live in India because they cannot return home, and the homes they left have been destroyed.

To imagine what such a thing would mean to you, try to visualize a massive and brutal military thrusting itself into your country by sheer force of numbers, destroying everything of value to you, pillaging your country from one border to the other, forcing you to live as it desires, and punishing you violently if you resist. Every church has been looted or destroyed. Every priest and nun has been forced to renounce his or her religion, flee the country, or be killed. For almost half a century an alien nation has imposed itself, its culture, its laws, and its prejudices upon you and while the world watches, no one has come forward to help.

I am telling you this history because of a story the Dalai Lama related to a group of students at Harvard. He told them of recently speaking to a monk who had spent eighteen years in a Chinese prison. During their conversation the monk mentioned that there were times he had been in danger. "What kind of danger?" the Dalai Lama asked, to which the monk replied, "Danger of losing my compassion for the Chinese."

When you think of "terrorists" or remember the Twin Towers collapsing with thousands of people inside, are you in danger of losing your compassion? When you fear that someone will attack you because you are not like them, are you in danger of losing your compassion? If so, you will become like them—a rigid person who sees "enemies" and has no compassion for them. That is the greatest danger we face.

It takes courage to fight a war in a dry and cold desert, but how dry and cold is your heart when you hate, when you need revenge, when you want someone to die? That is the desert in which you will fight your greatest battle and, if you are brave enough, win it.

Finding the Path

THE COMMON DESTINATION

The event had ended, everyone was tired but grateful, and our post-event staff circle was coming to an end. One of the facilitators, trying to think clearly after five days of intense emotional involvement with ninety people, lost track of her thought.

"Where am I going?" she asked herself out loud. Without pausing, she answered in a way that no one, including her, expected.

"I am going where everyone is going," she said with authority.

Her answer suddenly shifted all of us into an awareness of our mortality.

We are all going to die. That is our common destination. We are fellow sailors on the way to the same port. How long the voyage will last is different for all. It is for each of us to decide how we shall make the voyage, and what we shall gain from it.

Some travelers will learn from everything that happens along the way, change because of what they have learned, and arrive quite different from what they were when they started. Others will complain throughout the voyage, criticize their fellow travelers, and arrive at the final destination still angry, jealous, vengeful, avaricious, and frightened.

The voyage is an opportunity. How you use the opportunity is up to you. That is the choice that you must make at each moment. What you choose at each moment moves you along on your journey through the Earth school.

Sooner or later you will reach the end of that journey. Will you arrive grateful and wise, caring for your fellow travelers and receiving the care that they have for you, or will you arrive complaining about them and about the trip?

THE MISERY IS OPTIONAL

The story of a young man who died of AIDS is still in my mind. It will always be in my heart.

In many ways his life began when he learned of his diagnosis. After crying for a while, he called an older friend and mentor.

"What can I do?" he asked.

The friend said gently and firmly, "I have only one thing to recommend that you consider: Quality of Life."

That is what the young man did. In that process, he became a compassionate, caring, and courageous presence on the Earth. He endeavored to ignite compassion in those around him. He challenged those who disagreed with him, but always with care and respect. He strove to make his inner experience, day by day, an experience of quality. It is clear by the life that he lived between the time that he learned that he had AIDS and the time that he died that he was successful.

Many of the things that he said, in his unassuming way, brought me to an inner examination of my own quality of life.

"Are you beautiful or not?" he once asked, simply and directly. There was no way to avoid his question. It touched me and all who heard it. I still ask myself that question because my own quality of life depends upon the answer that I give.

As the disease progressed from intermittent discomfort to a continual experience of pain inside an emaciated body, he became even more clear about the inner dynamics that he had discovered, and that he was using to create his experiences.

"The pain is inevitable," he said, "but the misery is optional."

He experienced pain, but it seemed to me that, even in his most vulnerable times, he did not experience misery. In fact, it seemed to me that in his most vulnerable times he was his strongest, clearest, and most caring.

"In fifty years AIDS will be not be an issue," he said. "There will be other diseases by then. The question is, will we be able to treat the people who have them with compassion?"

Is this young man's life different from your own? You, also, will die, and you, also, will choose a response to this realization, whether you want to or not. Can you think of a better response than to turn your attention onto the quality of your life?

A life of quality is a life of care for other people, a life of integrity, and a life of receiving as well as giving. It is a life lived consciously, courageously, compassionately, and wisely. This young man looked at his mortality clearly, and used what he saw to transform his life.

That is what you were born to do, too.

LOVING THE TRUTH

It had been the most difficult retreat yet. Not because there were more people, which there were. Not because difficulties arose in communication, which they always do. This retreat was the first one that we had created after I had been appearing on *The Oprah Winfrey Show* for more than a year.

Many people came because they had seen me on television. Some had not read my books. They came because they were touched by what they heard Oprah and me discuss, but they had no way of knowing how difficult spiritual partnership can be and how deep the waters are that it stirs.

Expectations were abundant, and so was the frustration of not having them met. During one stressful moment, when a participant in the circle who had already spoken more than anyone else was speaking in general terms yet again, one of the facilitators interrupted her.

"Excuse me," she began softly. "Will you please use the word *I* instead of *we* when you speak? You say that 'We are all frustrated when our families don't understand us, and we don't know if we can bear the pain of that any longer.' You are not speaking for me, because I don't feel that way. Would you please try saying, 'I am frustrated when my family doesn't understand me, and I don't know if I can bear the pain of that any longer'?"

Reluctantly, the woman reworded her statement, and immediately she began to weep. No one spoke. We felt her pain and suffered with her.

After the retreat, as the staff sat in a circle of its own, the facilitator who interrupted the young woman sat quietly, apparently deep in her thoughts. At last, she said, "It was very difficult for me to listen to that young woman speak again without revealing anything about herself. I don't know why, but I could barely stand it. At last, I had to speak, and I am glad that I did. It made me see something new about myself. Before, I always listened to people, and made myself needed by doing that.

"Now," she said, "I love the truth more than I need to be loved."

We knew that she spoke a truth and we knew she would never be the same because of it.

Do you love the truth more than you need to be loved, or do you need to be loved more than you love the truth? Can you find what is true for you and share it with sensitivity? Learning how to do that is the path that each of us is on. No one can get off the path. The path is your life. The only question is how long you will walk on the path before you realize where it is leading you, and appreciate what is on it.

PART TWO

Soul Questions

Exploring Soul Questions

Soul questions come from a deeper place than other questions in our lives. They reach toward meaning and fulfillment. When you are thirsty you look for the well. The thirstier you are, the more important the well becomes to you. Soul questions come from deep thirst, even if it is not recognized. They do not concern themselves with the functional aspects of a life, such as projects and careers. They cannot be answered with numbers or theories. Soul questions come from beyond the intellect and the answers to them reach beyond the intellect. Soul questions are asked and answered soul to soul. They are doorways through which soul-to-soul communication enters your life and transforms it.

"How can I love?" "What is the purpose of my life?" "How can I change?" and "Why must I feel such pain?" are soul questions. There are as many soul questions as there are souls, but all have in common the longing for a vertical path through life—for transformation, deeper meaning, fulfillment, and love—rather than a horizontal path—more of the same in different guises. More anger, more success, more recognition, more wealth, more influence, more disdain, etc. Soul questions are about changing yourself instead of changing others. That is a way of saying that soul questions are a part of the pursuit of authentic power. They are inquiries into health and wholeness. As your soul questions are answered to your satisfaction, others appear and general or theoretical questions, such as, "Why is there Life?" and "Why is there suffering?" are replaced with immediate questions such as, "How can I use this experience to grow spiritually?" and "What can I do to challenge and change my anger, or need to please, in *this* circumstance?"

As you experiment with the answers you receive, you begin to see which of them are valuable to you and which are not, which nurture you and which deplete you. Your answers may appear to come from a holy text, a wise friend, or a helpful book, but they do not. Answers that nurture you come from the Universe, and you recognize them by your resonance when you hear, read, or have an intuition about them. Then it is for you to decide whether or not to pay attention to them, to apply them in your life and see what they produce. Do they make you humbler, clearer, more forgiving, or loving? If so, continue to apply them and experiment with them. If not, ask your questions again.

Every soul-to-soul communication benefits all souls. Personalities have different challenges, but all souls have the same intentions—harmony, cooperation, sharing, and reverence for Life. Perhaps you have already asked some of the questions in this book. Perhaps some of them will inspire you to ask other soul questions and to open yourself to the answers. That is the purpose of soul questions: to deepen your experiences and open yourself to them again and again until all that is left is the power and beauty of the life you are creating and giving to others.

You may find in the following soul questions some of the ideas and insights that you encountered in Part One. This is appropriate, just as recognizing recurring words and phrases is necessary to learning a new language. And just as a new language gives you new freedom of expression and insight, the new perceptions that are becoming central to the human experience and the new vocabulary that accompanies them will allow you to explore in new and surprising ways your own experiences and the depth, power, and meaning of your life.

Now let's explore some soul questions.

Exploring
Fundamentals

HOW DO YOU KNOW?

What is your philosophy based on? How do we know what you wrote is only an illusion/fantasy or whether it has value?

"How do you know what you know?" is as difficult to answer as the question, "Where does Life come from?" I pay attention to my experiences. I listen to my inner sense of what is worth listening to. When I feel it, I make a point of remembering what I have heard and applying it to see if it works for me. You have the same ability. Something I have said or written has caught your attention. Now you want to know more about it.

What did that experience feel like? Pay attention to it. Something happened within you that causes you to seek the source of my insights—insights that you recognized. When you recognized my insights, they became your insights. If you say to yourself or others that they come from me, you miss the point. That is like saying what you see in a mirror originates in the mirror. In fact, when you look into a mirror you see only your reflection. When you recognize wisdom, wherever or however that happens for you, it is your wisdom that is being reflected back to you. Then you must decide whether to trust what you recognize. Will you look outside of yourself to make that decision, or inside? That is the question.

Rejecting—for any reason—what you recognize to be significant for you invalidates your own experience, your own power, and the impulses of your own heart. I suggest that you decide for yourself whether what stirs you is worthy of your interest. Do not look for footnotes in matters of the heart and soul. Look inside yourself. Otherwise, you will always be looking for references and longing to know from others how they know what they know.

WHAT IS THE SOURCE OF YOUR INFORMATION?
Do your ideas come from Buddhist, Christian, or Sufi traditions?

I am often asked if the ideas that I share come from Buddhist, or Muslim, or Hindu, or Christian sources, and what books have influenced me.

Nothing that I write or speak about comes from a book or a religion. The ideas come from the Universe. They are not mine. If I did not write about them, other people would, and other people are. Soon many more people will write about them, also. That is because a new species is being born inside each of us, no matter where we live, what language we speak, or what we do. I strive to provide a vocabulary for this new species. Eventually, we will all express the new perceptions and values of this new species.

Mahatma Gandhi called his autobiography *My Experiments with Truth.* "Mahatma" means "Great Soul." When you begin to use your life as an experiment with truth, you put yourself on the same road. The species that is being born is a species of great souls. We are those great souls—every one of us on this precious Earth.

I also experiment with truth. When I hear something that I recognize as true for me, I try it out. If it works, I incorporate it into my life and I use it. You can do the same thing. In fact, it is important that you do. Your evolution and the evolution of our species now depends upon it.

It is easy to do. If you recognize something that I write, for example, as true for you, what you recognize becomes your truth at that moment. Your recognition makes it your truth. From that time onward you do not need to refer to me as the source. The Universe is the source and you are the recipient. You become the authority in your life. Other people do the same thing. They use their authority to accept from you what they recognize as true for themselves. At that moment, they become the source of that truth, and so on.

We are in the process of becoming wise. This is one of the ways that it happens.

DO I NEED A TEACHER?

I have many guides, many. But I believe I do actually need help and guidance from another. Not a guru, not a God, but a teacher.

I love listening to the stories my adopted Sioux uncle tells me. I always find so much wisdom in them, even when I have heard them many times before—especially when I have heard them many times before. They are stories of valor, tenderness, kindness, and relationship. They are always appropriate, and always told as if I hadn't asked him a question, if I did ask him a question. Sometimes he tells me stories when I haven't asked him a question and, to my surprise, they answer questions that I didn't realize I was asking.

Recently my uncle visited his boyhood home on the Standing Rock reservation where he grew up over seventy-five years ago.

"Nephew," he told me, wiping his tears, "all of the old people are gone. I still have questions, but there's no one left to answer them. I've got to find the answers myself now."

My uncle had become an elder. I always looked at him that way, but now he did, too. He didn't have anyone to answer his questions, or the questions that I and others ask him. He didn't stop answering my questions, through his stories, but when he couldn't draw upon what the old people told him, he prayed to the Creator and went deep within himself to find the answer.

We are reaching this place as a species. We are learning to draw upon ourselves for the answers that we need, not because the old people are gone but because what worked in the past no longer works. Old ways now lead only to painful consequences.

We need to become our own authorities now, as my uncle did, and to treat each other kindly as we each learn how to do this.

That means we are becoming teachers to ourselves and each other. It is now our responsibility to learn how to feel, to listen from the heart, to share from the heart, and to cocreate in spiritual partnership—partnership between equals for the purpose of spiritual growth.

Becoming your own authority does not mean relinquishing the necessity, comfort, and fulfillment of having Teachers. It means finding them inside of yourself, and learning to value what you hear and see. It also means seeing the world around you as a teacher, and learning to value what you hear and see. When you do these things, you begin the process of becoming an elder.

We are all becoming elders together.

WHAT IS EVIL?

What is the distinction between recognizing something evil and judging it?

Evil is an absence. It is not a presence. Evil is the absence of Love—uncontaminated conscious Light. The remedy for an absence is a presence, not an action. You cannot imprison, deport, or kill evil. Not even a great army can defeat evil. It can only defeat another army.

Where there is an absence of Love there is fear, judgment, and violence. If you fear and judge the darkness, you step into the darkness. Evil is the darkness. You cannot fight evil without joining it. You cannot judge it without joining it. You can recognize it without joining it. The difference between judgment of evil and recognition of evil is your emotional reaction. If you are repulsed and frightened, you are judging what you encounter. If you can see an angry, or deceitful, or violent person for what he or she is—a fellow student in the Earth school who is in extreme pain—you can interact with that person appropriately. You do not need to trust her with your savings. You also do not need to feel superior or righteous.

When you have an emotional reaction to what you see, you are judging. That is your signal that you have an issue inside of yourself—with yourself—not with the other person. If you react self-righteously to evil, look inside yourself for the very thing that so agitates you, and you will find it. If it were not there, you would simply discern, act appropriately, and move on. When you have an emotional reaction to evil—the absence of Love—that absence is in you. Understanding this is very important because it enables you to personally contribute to the reduction of evil. You do that by changing yourself into the loving person that you would like others to be. Until you do, you will be a part of the evil that so repulses you.

The change from an absence of Love in a human life to the presence of Love in a human life is the creation of authentic power—the alignment of the personality with the soul. Your emotional reactions to the evil you encounter and your judgments of it show you what you need to change in yourself. Changing those parts of your personality that judge, react in fear, and cannot love into acceptance, fearlessness, and love is the journey you were born to make.

WHAT EXACTLY IS REINCARNATION?

Many of us have been taught that when we were born each of us was a new person with a new soul. Your views are based on the concept of reincarnation, so it is important for us to understand it.

Every night you sleep, and the next morning you wake up. If you had an argument with your friend yesterday, you will still have the consequences of that argument to face when you wake up. They don't disappear because you went to sleep. You will still be responsible tomorrow for what you did today.

Reincarnation is just like that. What you create will be there for you to face in your next life if you don't take care of it in this one, just like the consequences that you create today will be waiting for you tomorrow if you don't take care of them before you go to bed. You are always responsible for what you do and your responsibility cannot be assumed by anyone else.

When you die, you don't go to sleep. You go home and you are very much awake. You are also a much larger you than you are now. That is your soul. The consequences that you created but didn't experience before you died do not disappear. They are waiting for you. You may think that you do not want to deal with them, but your larger you—your soul—does. In fact, it creates another lifetime just to do that.

Once you start to look at things this way, you begin to do things differently. You treat people the way that you would like to be treated yourself. That is the Golden Rule. You don't have to be a Christian to appreciate the Golden Rule. Billions of Hindus and Buddhists, who believe in reincarnation, understand exactly what it means.

Reincarnation is a compassionate way of learning responsibility. You do not suffer for eternity because you do the wrong thing once, or twice, or even time after time. It is not possible to do a wrong thing. You do what you do and you experience the consequences of what you do. It's that simple. If you don't experience those consequences before you die, your soul creates another life so that you can. That is reincarnation.

Eventually you begin to treat other people the way that you want to be treated. That means you change in big ways. You put yourself in your brother's shoes before you speak or act. You let yourself feel your sister's pain. You become more tender and caring. You also become more wise.

Maybe you will make those big changes in this lifetime. You can, if you want to. Maybe you will take many lifetimes. Sooner or later, you will make them. When you become completely loving and kind—without fear and without thought of harming others—you graduate from the Earth school.

That is when reincarnation ends.

CAN YOU PROVE THAT LIFE EXISTS AFTER DEATH?
What physical proof do you have of life after death?

It is not possible to provide evidence of life after death to the five senses any more than it is possible to provide the five senses with evidence of nonphysical reality. It cannot be done. The five senses—taste, touch, sight, hearing, and smell—together form a single sensory system whose object of detection is physical reality. This sensory system cannot detect nonphysical reality.

Humankind is now moving beyond the limitations of the five senses. It is becoming able to access data that the five senses cannot provide and to utilize that data consciously. In other words, it is becoming highly intuitive. This is multisensory perception. Multisensory perception does not replace five-sensory perception. It adds to it. Multisensory humans perceive physical circumstances, but they also see meaning in them that five-sensory humans do not. Multisensory humans do not deduce or conclude meaning in their five-sensory circumstances. They perceive it directly.

Multisensory humans feel what is appropriate for themselves regardless of what their five senses tell them and their intellects conclude. Learning to use multisensory perception does not require faith. It requires the openness to experiment with your inner sense of knowing when you feel it. Your inner sense of knowing is your access to nonphysical reality. Nonphysical reality is your home. It is where you came from when you were born and where you will return when you die. It has no color, taste, sound, fragrance, or sensation. It is much more, just as the world outside a school building is much more than can be contained in any of its classrooms. You cannot prove, without leaving a classroom, or the ability to look outside of it, that anything outside of the classroom exists.

WHAT DO YOU MEAN BY "UNIVERSE"?

Do you use the word "Universe" to mean God? I never hear you use the word "God."

I use the word "Universe" to refer to Divine Intelligence—to the living, boundless Universe of compassion and wisdom. If that is your definition of God, we are talking about the same thing.

DOES THE UNIVERSE CARE ABOUT US?

If the Earth school ceases to exist due to a natural disaster of some kind, would the rest of this vast Universe even care, or be aware of it?

There is only one Universe. It is not really accurate to think of all the parts of the Universe as "connected." They are more than connected. They are One. If you cut your finger, do you hurt? If you break your toe, do you hurt? If you have a headache, do you hurt? Whenever a part of your body hurts, wherever that part is, you hurt. That is how intimately bound to the Universe you are. What you say, what you choose, and what you shape your personality to be with your choices is important. Everything in the Earth school is important. Do not deceive yourself into thinking that our precious Earth is an orphan no one loves. The Universe is alive, wise, and compassionate. No thought is unheard and no prayer goes unanswered, although not always in the way that you expect.

DO WE HAVE A DESTINY?

If the Universe determines my destiny, what role do I play in shaping my fate?

The Universe does not burden you with a destiny. It provides you with potential. How much of that potential you realize depends upon the choices that you make. At each moment you are given an opportunity to choose. What you choose leads you to more choices. Each of those choices leads you to yet more choices, and so on.

For example, a person who speaks rudely to you gives you an opportunity to choose how you will respond. Will you withdraw emotionally? Will you become angry? Will you be able to see his or her fear and pain and respond appropriately? The choice is always yours—whether the issue is a rude person, the death of a friend, losing a job, or missing the bus. When you make a choice you pass through one of several doorways. The rest of the doorways close and you are again presented with more choices— more doorways. In each instance, one of the choices available to you is the optimal choice. The optimal choice that you can make in any situation is to grow spiritually.

Moment by moment you are presented with an array of choices, one of which is optimal, no matter what you previously chose. There is wisdom in each of your choices because each of them creates consequences that you will experience, and, if you choose, learn from.

Your path through the Earth school is determined choice by choice—your choices, not the Universe's.

WHY ARE THOUGHTS POWERFUL?
How do thoughts create? Why are they powerful?

Thoughts open you or close you. The thought that you might not be able to pay your rent closes you. The thought that the Universe is your friend opens you. The thought that your marriage might dissolve closes you. The thought that you are your own source of well-being opens you. What your thoughts open or close you to is your experience. They determine whether you will fear and resist your experiences, or whether you will embrace them and be supported by them.

Choosing your thoughts is like choosing a pair of glasses. One pair is dark gray. They make everything appear threatening. Their lenses have built-in distortions that twist everything that you see. When you wear them, all of your experiences are frightening. Another pair gives everything that you see a comforting, golden glow. Their lenses do not distort, but help you to see more clearly. When you wear these glasses, all of your experiences appear friendly.

There are many other kinds of glasses. Some distort and color your vision more than others, and some distort and color it less. Each frightening thought does the same thing that a dark and distorting pair of glasses does. It makes what you see appear to be threatening. Every grateful and loving thought does what a light and clear pair of glasses does. It brightens what you see and reveals the beauty around you.

For example, if you get sick and can't go on a trip that you planned, your illness will appear as a disaster if you think only about the vacation time you are losing, or if you think that the only way you can enjoy yourself is to go somewhere else. It will appear as a gift if you think about what your illness and staying at home can show you about yourself that is important for you to know. The illness is the same in both cases. The lost vacation time and the stay at home are the same, too. The thought that you choose when you think about them is what determines your experience.

A reporter once asked a monk from Tibet, "Why are you always so optimistic? Your country is occupied by a foreign army and you may never be able to see your family again."

"Because," said the monk, "it makes me feel good."

This monk knew how to choose his glasses—his thoughts—deliberately.

What thoughts are you choosing?

WHAT IS NEW ABOUT MULTISENSORY PERCEPTION?

Multisensory perception apparently does not exclude the products of thought and inference—so what makes it so new?

Multisensory perception is the ability to obtain data that the five senses cannot provide. The five senses cannot tell you which bus to take in order to sit next to a future colleague who will stimulate you to greater insights and achievements. Multisensory perception can, for example, in the form of a hunch to take one bus instead of the other.

Your five senses cannot tell you which individual, among many who appear generous, is not generous. Multisensory perception can.

Your five senses cannot provide you with an experience of the Universe as alive, wise, and compassionate. Multisensory perception can.

The entire human species is now becoming multisensory. This transformation is occurring very fast from an evolutionary perspective. In a few generations the human experience will be very different from what it is now. The experience of what it means to be a female and what it means to be a male are already changing dramatically.

Multisensory perception is replacing rational analysis as the primary decision-making tool in millions of humans. Humanity is becoming a heart-centered species instead of a head-centered species. We are beginning to see power as the alignment of the personality with the soul instead of the ability to manipulate and control.

We have always had multisensory humans among us. Now everyone is becoming multisensory.

That is new.

WHAT IS THE BASIS FOR THE EARTH SCHOOL CONCEPT?

I am intrigued by your concept of an Earth school. Where did you get it?

The Earth school is not a concept. The Earth school is an ongoing three-dimensional, full-color, high-fidelity, interactive, multimedia experience that does not end until your soul goes home—until you die. Every moment in the Earth school offers you an opportunity to learn important things about yourself. Those things have to do with your soul. The Earth school operates with exquisite perfection and perfect efficiency whether you are aware of it or not. The Earth school does not test you and you cannot fail it. It continually offers you opportunities to grow in wisdom and compassion. I suggest that you experiment with the possibility that the Earth school is a learning environment that continually presents you with circumstances that are perfect for your spiritual growth, and see what that experiment produces in your life.

Becoming a
Spiritual Person

WHAT DO YOU MEAN BY "SPIRITUAL"?

What does "spiritual" really mean?

Spiritual means having to do with your soul. When you focus your attention on creating with the intentions of your soul, your endeavors become spiritual. The intentions of your soul are harmony, cooperation, sharing, and reverence for Life. When those intentions become your intentions, your personality is aligned with your soul. That is authentic power.

Authentic power is the experience of being grateful to be alive, even during difficult experiences. Your life is filled with meaning and purpose. Your creativity is unlimited. You enjoy yourself and others. You are fulfilled and fulfilling. You treasure Life in all its forms.

Becoming a spiritual person requires becoming aware of your emotions. It also requires consciousness of your intentions, and taking responsibility for your choices.

You were born to be a spiritual person.

WHAT DO YOU MEAN BY "INNER WORK"?

You often say that a person has to do the work to change and to create a more compassionate self and world. Could you better define what you mean by "work"?

The first step is to become aware of your fears, such as anger and jealousy. You may think that you are aware of all of them now, but look deeper. Beneath anger, for example, is physical pain. It is easier to become angry with someone else, or yourself, or the Universe, than to feel this pain. That pain is a direct, unfiltered experience of fear. Simply recognizing when you are angry is not enough. You must go to the root of the emotion, which is a part of your personality that you do not know about, or are too frightened or ashamed of to acknowledge.

Once you become familiar with an emotion in terms of its physical sensations, you will not need to label it as "anger," "jealousy," or "fear." You will recognize how your body feels when it comes and what thoughts fill your mind. Then you will be able to see it as an old acquaintance with whom you have a disagreement. This is the disagreement: You do not want to feel the way that it does. This is where challenging the frightened parts of your personality comes in.

Challenging a frightened part of your personality is not a declaration of war. It is a clear statement of your intention. "I challenge this experience. I no longer want it in my energy system," is an example. Challenging a frightened part of your personality is the decision to use your free will to change an aspect of yourself that you do not want to be creating experiences in your life anymore. It is realizing that if you do not challenge your anger—or fear or jealousy—you will die with it.

Growing older does not mean automatically becoming gentler or wiser. Millions of people die angry, frightened, and jealous. If you do not change yourself, you will be one of them. No one can change you except yourself.

You challenge a frightened part of your personality by choosing not to behave as you habitually have in the past when this part of your personality became active. When you feel impatient, for example, you can choose to stop and consider the other person's needs instead of your own. When you become angry you can choose not to shout if you usually shout, or not to withdraw emotionally if you usually do that. When you feel the need to say yes in order to please, you can say no instead if that is what you really want to say.

No matter how you do it, recognizing and challenging frightened parts of your personality that you want to change, and recognizing and cultivating loving parts of your personality that you want to strengthen, are the heart of spiritual growth. You cannot be a spiritually evolved person and an emotionally unevolved person at the same time.

WHAT ARE THE FIRST STEPS OF SPIRITUAL GROWTH?

What are the first steps I should take to begin to explore my spirituality?

Start by becoming aware of your emotions. You cannot become spiritually advanced while you are unaware of what you are feeling. Emotional awareness requires you to become conscious of everything you are feeling all the time. It is difficult to become emotionally aware because many of your emotions are painful—but your painful emotions offer you the opportunities you need to grow spiritually because they originate in the frightened parts of your personality that you need to locate, challenge, and heal in order to grow into your full potential.

WHAT IS THE ROLE OF SACRED PRACTICES IN SPIRITUAL DEVELOPMENT?

What is the role of sacred practices, such as meditation, movement, and prayer, in spiritual development?

Every form of Life is sacred. Therefore it is impossible to have an activity that is not sacred. The Universe is sacred. You are sacred and all that you do is sacred. The life of each individual is a sacred practice, although he or she may not be aware of it.

When you take time to know yourself, or to appreciate your life and the lives of others, you open yourself to the experience of the sacred. You do the same thing when you pray. The more you open yourself to the experience of the sacred the more you see that is sacred. Eventually, you see that everything is sacred.

Coming to see everything as sacred and honoring the sacred everywhere you see it is spiritual development.

WHAT DOES THE SCIENTIFIC METHOD HAVE TO DO WITH SPIRITUALITY?

If we replace the scientific method with other ways of knowing, how will we replace the certainty that science provides?

The type of certainty that the scientific method provides can help you to survive. It cannot help you to grow spiritually. The statistical predictions of the quantum theory can be useful in designing nuclear power plants, but they cannot assist you or anyone else in experiencing your most painful emotions, discovering their origins, and healing them. They also cannot help you to give the gifts that you were born to give.

The scientific method is a product of five-sensory humanity— individuals who are limited in their perception to what their eyes, ears, nose, skin, and tongue can reveal to them. Now all of humankind is becoming multisensory. We are becoming aware of ourselves as more than minds and bodies, muscles and organs, hormones and neurotransmitters. Our goal is no longer survival, but spiritual growth. That requires the development of inner knowing and inner authority. It requires the heart, not the intellect.

You cannot calculate whether the job, partner, or life step that you are considering is the correct one for you. It may be appropriate for others, but that is beside the point. The point is that only you are living your life and only you will experience the consequences of your choices as immediately and intimately.

How will you assess possibilities? With your head or with your heart? Authentic power is the development of the ability to speak, act, and live with the certainty that your words, actions, and life are appropriate while at the same time allowing others to do the same.

This is a certainty that does not need to be replicated or validated by others.

WHY STRIVE FOR SPIRITUAL GROWTH IF THE WORLD IS COMING TO AN END?

I have heard many prophecies that natural disasters and global economic problems will increase and destroy us. What's the point of trying to grow spiritually if our destiny has already been written?

No one's destiny has been written. You are born with potential, not a limited destiny. Whether or not you reach the fullest potential that is available to you is a matter of the choices that you make. At any moment you can leave the life path that you are now on and embark on one that is more compassionate, wise, fulfilling, and free. Not even your nonphysical Teachers know what you will choose in your tomorrows. Why squander your moments exploring the what-ifs of your life? They are endless and unlimited.

Your consciousness is more powerful than you think. If you apply your consciousness to the consideration of unavoidable and catastrophic events, you contribute to their creation. If you apply it to the consideration of a world that is based on the intentions of your soul, you contribute to the creation of that, too. The most fundamental choice that you face, moment by moment, is how you will learn wisdom—through fear and doubt or through love and trust. This is the eternal question. It is the Garden of Eden question. It is the longest-running show on Broadway.

Our ecological and economic problems are real. So are the fear and greed that created them. Spiritual growth requires locating and healing that fear and greed in you. It is making the connection between your internal experiences and your external experiences. That connection is this: Your external experiences reflect your internal experiences. What is behind your eyes is

more important than what is in front of them. You cannot change
the reflection in a mirror without changing what the mirror reflects. The mirror is the world that you live in, and it reflects you.
If you fear the future and doubt that it can be changed, you have
chosen to learn wisdom through fear and doubt. This is a painful
way to learn.

Learning wisdom through love and trust is a different experience. It requires inner work. There is only one place you can do
this work—in yourself. That is how you change what the mirror
reflects.

That is also spiritual growth.

Relating to Others

DO YOU BELIEVE IN SOUL MATES?

What do I do when a soul mate shows up and I am already in a relationship?

Every individual that you have encountered or will encounter is your soul mate. Each human is a soul that has voluntarily entered the Earth school in order to experience certain circumstances and to contribute certain gifts. Incarnation is a dramatic act of spiritual responsibility. It is a path that you have chosen and that everyone you have met or will meet has chosen.

Your challenge is to determine how you will relate with the millions of soul mates that you will encounter in the course of your lifetime. The relationships that you now have are with fellow souls. The relationships that you will form in the future will also be with fellow souls. Relationships illuminate parts of your personality that are unhealed—such as the parts that dominate others, please others, judge others, and exploit them. Changing your relationships will not heal those parts of yourself. Your new relationships will continue to illuminate the same unhealed parts in you until you heal them.

If you are in a relationship and "fall in love" with someone else, for example, or think that you have found the one and only person you were destined to be with, or who will complete you, or fulfill you, ask yourself if you are running from the issues that have surfaced in your current relationship. Is the idea of a new relationship affecting you the way that an anesthetic affects an individual in physical pain? Is it exhilarating or euphoric? Is it keeping you from the experience of very real and difficult issues in your life? Until you find and heal the frightened parts of your personality that created these issues, you will re-create them in your next relationship.

In other words, changing relationships without coming to terms with the parts of your personality that created the relationship is like changing props on a stage. The play continues. Only the scenery is different. When you heal a part of your personality, the play changes. You no longer need an abusive relationship, or a dependent one. You no longer need to dominate another, or to be submissive to another. That part of your journey is complete. Other paths open to you, with different requirements than the previous path.

Your soul mates are not your saviors. They are your fellow students in the Earth school.

HOW CAN I LET GO OF MY EXPECTATIONS OF OTHERS?

Why is letting go of my expectations so difficult?

Shift your attention from others to what you feel when you interact with others. When you have expectations and they are met, notice what you feel. Notice also what you feel when your expectations are not met. The most effective way to do this is to notice what you are feeling without speaking or acting.

If you can resist the impulse to criticize, object, explain, clarify, withdraw, or become angry, you will be surprised at how powerful and painful some of the physical sensations in your body are. The more proficient you become at feeling these sensations, observing them, and learning about them, the less interested you will be in diverting your attention from them by shouting, withdrawing, judging, and all of the other ways that you have used in the past.

This is how to develop emotional awareness. Eventually your emotions will become more interesting to you than what appears to cause them. When that happens, your expectations will disappear naturally, and you will not even notice that they are gone.

HOW CAN I FORGIVE SOMEONE WHO BETRAYS ME AGAIN AND AGAIN?

The people that I forgive are not always worthy of my trust and take advantage of my forgiveness. Afterward, I feel foolish and angry at them and myself. I try again and forgive, and once again am devastated when I am deceived or manipulated. How can I forgive a loved one when I realize that he continues to betray my trust?

It is not possible for someone to take advantage of your forgiveness. Forgiveness does not have anything to do with other people. It has everything to do with you.

Forgiveness is letting go of your resentment, disappointment, anger, and hurt. When you do, you are free from these prisons. They no longer captivate your attention. They no longer intrude on your thoughts and your sleep. You are no longer steeped in anger and righteous indignation. You no longer feel the need to convince others that you have been wronged. You give up being a victim and step into a lighter, less restricted consciousness.

Forgiveness is self-healing. Before you forgive, you are fixated on what has not gone the way that you wanted it to go. Not forgiving is holding on to your expectations. Forgiving is releasing them.

The feeling of being betrayed by someone that you have forgiven is not as simple a matter as it appears, but once you understand that your expectations are involved, it becomes much clearer. When you feel that you have been betrayed by someone, it is because you have expectations about that person that he or she did not fulfill. Forgiving means letting go of those expectations. Once you do that, there is nothing for anyone to betray, and no way that you can feel betrayed.

If you say to yourself that you have forgiven someone, but you haven't let go of your expectations, your forgiveness is not really forgiveness. It is an attempt to manipulate that person into behaving in a way that is acceptable to you. When he or she doesn't do that, you feel betrayed. It is really the failure of your attempt to manipulate that hurts. You wanted something to happen, and it didn't. Not forgiving is insisting that another person be the way that you want him or her to be. Forgiving is letting go of that insistence. It allows you to see clearly, instead of through the filters of your desires.

Once you see clearly, you can act appropriately. If that requires that you change your relationships, you can do that with an open heart. You do not have to resent someone in order to make a change in your life. You can do it because it is appropriate, because you see changes that you want to make, and you make them.

Here is the main point: If you forgive, but continue to resent, you have not forgiven. If you forgive, but tell others how happy you are to be done with the ordeal, you have not forgiven. If your heart is not light and joyful, you have not forgiven.

Forgiving is choosing a light and joyful heart instead of anger and resentment. Anger and resentment are very attractive. You cannot be a victim without them. You cannot live with a light and happy heart and be a victim at the same time.

The choice is yours.

WHY CAN'T I FALL IN LOVE?

I feel complete (and not needy) but can never seem to fall for anyone.
Why is this?

Love is not something you fall into. It must be cultivated and developed. It requires patience and dedication. It is your ability to care about others. It is not a sentimental feeling. It is experiencing your deep connection with all of Life. It is your ability to feel the pain of others and the joy of others. It is also appreciating Life and desiring to contribute to it. As you begin to look at love and your life in this way you will not be so concerned about "falling in love," yet at the same time you will find your life filling with love.

HOW CAN I LOVE WITHOUT FEAR?

I am struggling to love my partner without fears or expectations,
but I am finding that despite the fact that I can love others without
fear, I am unable to love her that way.

Love and fear exclude each other. You cannot love and fear at the same time. You also cannot fear and love at the same time. There are times when you love your partner. Those are the times when you want to support her. You delight in her growing strength. Her vulnerabilities bring out your most caring tenderness. This is how we were meant to be with each other. It is natural to love.

There are also times when you are frightened. You fear what he will say or do next, or what you will say or do. You want to remain together and you are frightened that you will separate. You fear that you will not be able to give him what he needs, or that he will not be able to do that for you.

It may be that you are able to love others more consistently because they are not close enough to you to stimulate your fears the way that your partner does. This is good. Spiritual partnership is partnership between equals for the purpose of spiritual growth. Spiritual growth requires finding and healing the frightened parts of your personality. If your partnership didn't activate these parts it couldn't help you to grow spiritually.

You are together to learn how to love. Your fears show you what you need to work on. They are what needs to be changed in yourself. You know that your spiritual partnership is working when it activates frightened parts of your personality. It would not be working if it didn't.

Eventually you will learn to love each other and, in the process, everyone and everything. Before that happens, you will encounter all of the frightened parts of your personality. That is the first step in healing them.

WHAT IS THE DIFFERENCE BETWEEN JUDGING AND DISCERNING?

Is discerning something in another person and judging another person the same thing?

Judgment is accompanied by a negative emotional reaction. You do not like what you see. You resist what you experience. You would like a person or situation to be different. You have expectations that are not satisfied. When that happens, you lose energy.

Discerning is seeing a person or a circumstance as it is. You observe the behavior of another individual, or a quality in another individual, without a painful emotional reaction to your observation. You notice jealousy, for example, or anger, greed, or callousness in another person without being affected by it, just as you notice the color of a flower or the shape of a rock without being affected by it. You do not lose energy.

If you think you are discerning, check inside yourself. Do you resist what you see? Do you wish that an individual or circumstance were different? If so, you will discover that what you are feeling inside is painful. That painful experience is your signal that you are judging.

HOW CAN I PROTECT MYSELF WITHOUT BECOMING JUDGMENTAL?

I'm wondering how to react toward someone who lies, commits cruel acts toward his children, etc. What would you say to elderly people who are bilked out of their life savings by con men or to girls who are raped by their dates, who they thought were nice guys. How do I protect myself without becoming judgmental?

As we have said, judgment is not the same as discernment. Judging is seeing yourself as superior to another person. Discernment is seeing others clearly. When you judge, you create painful consequences for yourself. You cut yourself off from others, except those whom you judge worthy of your presence. You deprive yourself of the richness that the Universe continually offers you. Judging is like watching a big-screen, big-sound, full-color feature film in black and white on a tiny television set with one small speaker. The feature film is your life. The reduced black-and-white version of it is what you see through your judgments.

How can you best protect yourself—by seeing your world in large, clear, colorful detail, or by looking at a reduced, colorless image of it? Even if your world is painful in the extreme, and contains such things as the Holocaust, or slavery, or abuse as a child, which view gives you greater ability to assess what needs to be done and to do it as effectively as you can?

You can see deceitfulness and brutality without judging those who are deceitful and brutal. You can do more than that. You can use your experiences with brutality and deceitfulness to challenge the parts of your personality that insist on judging, and heal them.

Victor Frankl was put into a concentration camp by the Nazis.

The worst things imaginable happened to him. People that he loved were killed. He was tortured and everything that he had was taken from him. He labored in the bitter cold. He slept packed together with other people on boards in frozen barracks. There was just enough food to starve slowly.

One dark morning as his work party stumbled along a rocky road against an icy wind, with guards shouting and hitting them with the butts of their rifles, Victor realized something that changed his life. The ultimate and the highest goal to which he could aspire was love!

Victor did not collapse into the position of a victim, hating his persecutors and belittling himself. He stepped into the greatness of his soul. He did not say, "Why me?" or "This is unfair." When you say things like that, you have no power. He saw and felt the brutality of a concentration camp every day, but he did not judge it. Instead he said, "The salvation of man is through love and in love." He became a very powerful person, even in such terrible circumstances.

You can experience for yourself the difference between discernment and judgment. Judgment has an emotional charge to it. It makes one person a victim and another a villain. Your reactions are compulsive. You think that you have no choice. Discernment allows you to observe, analyze with your heart, and act accordingly.

Who needs protection—the one who judges, or the one who discerns?

HOW CAN I TELL A FRIEND ABOUT A FLAW?

How do I tell a friend he is too judgmental without hurting him?

Telling a friend that he is too judgmental is a judgment that you make about your friend. Your friend may not agree with your judgment. You have your idea about what defines a judgment, and he has his.

If you tell your friend what you feel in the moment, you do not judge him. For example, if you say, "When you speak to me like that, my stomach hurts," your friend cannot disagree. At the same time, you have shared some of your experience in a way that he might be able to hear. Since you are the authority on what you feel, he cannot argue when you say, "My stomach hurts." When you judge your friend, your judgment is as painful to him as his judgments are to you.

DO PEOPLE WHO IRRITATE ME REFLECT A PART OF ME?

Will you speak about people "mirroring" each other? If what another person does irritates me, is that a reflection of myself?

Yes. Your clue that there is something that you can learn about yourself from an interaction with another person is your emotional reaction to the interaction. When you do not want to see something about yourself, you will be irritated when you see it in others. This is "mirroring." For example, if you are irritated when you see someone who you think is selfish, conceited, and callous, look inside yourself for a part of you that is selfish, conceited, and callous. Try to remember a time when you spoke or acted in the same way. If you cannot remember such a time, keep looking.

When Linda and I were first together, I noticed that I became irritated when I felt she whined. I could not imagine myself as a whiner. I, who rode motorcycles, parachuted from airplanes, was a combat veteran and a former Green Beret officer, could not be a whiner. Nonetheless, I continued to watch myself for whining. Speaking with Linda one day I heard myself whine! It was startling, but unmistakable. I didn't like what she was saying and I was whining about it rather than telling her what I was feeling. From that moment onward I felt less and less irritated when it seemed to me that Linda was whining.

Becoming irritated when you see someone doing something that you do—but don't know that you are doing—is a well-known phenomenon. Psychologists call it "projection." You intensely dislike in others what you don't recognize, and don't want to recognize, in yourself. Finding in yourself the very behavior that you dislike in others is called "projection recall." When you do that, you bring your attention home. You see where the behavior that you find so objectionable really is. It is in you. Then the behavior no longer creates an emotional reaction in you when you encounter it in others. Paying attention to "mirroring" is an important part of spiritual growth. It requires becoming aware of everything that you are feeling, and learning about yourself from what you feel.

HOW CAN I AVOID BEING DRAWN INTO THE CHAOS OF OTHERS?

How can I remain "authentic" when others in my life try to draw me into their chaos?

Authentic power is the alignment of your personality with your soul. It is recognizing that you create moment by moment, and choosing to create wisely and compassionately. Creating authentic power requires responsible choice—a choice that creates consequences for which you are willing to accept responsibility. There is no place in this picture for a victim. A victim sees himself or herself at the mercy of others and attributes to others his or her state of consciousness, such as anger, jealousy, bliss, etc. Your friends are not necessarily attempting to draw you into their circumstances. They are being who they are. Their lives are as difficult and complex as your own. If you do not take your interactions so personally, you will be able to see that they offer you opportunities to resent others, become jealous of them, etc., and also opportunities to have compassion for them. In other words, you can see yourself as a victim who reacts to your circumstances or as a creator who chooses your response to the circumstances of your life.

Experiment with allowing yourself to choose your response the next time you feel drawn into the turbulence of others instead of reacting without awareness of your thoughts, feelings, and intention.

WHY DO CHILDREN AND PARENTS HAVE CONFLICTS?

What steps can I take to resolve conflicts with parents?

Conflicts with parents contain the most potential for spiritual growth. From a five-sensory perspective, parents are random people in your life, and so are children. From a multisensory perception, you and your parents agreed to the intimate parent-child bond before you were born. You and your parents are more than conflicting personalities. You are souls that are interacting by choice in the Earth school.

This is the case for every individual whose life touches your own. The relationship between children and parents, however, is particularly intense and fertile. You and your parents, and your siblings if you have any, chose one another before you were born because your struggles interlock and provide each of you the challenges that you require in order to find and heal parts of your personality that would keep you from your full potential if they were to remain unhealed.

Those unhealed parts of your personality are the origins of your most painful emotions. Your challenges with your parents—and theirs with you—are not random. You are each offering the other opportunities to grow spiritually. The issues that you have with your parents are precisely the issues that you must recognize and heal in yourself. You are each other's greatest gifts. The next time you judge a parent or feel judged by one, ask yourself, "What can I learn from this experience?" If you shift your attention from what is lacking in your parents to what your interactions with them can provide you to develop spiritually, you will begin to develop the very strengths that you need in order to give the gifts that you were born to give.

HOW CAN I TEACH MY CHILDREN TO BE NON-JUDGMENTAL?

How do I teach my children not to be judgmental? What can I say to eight- to ten-year-olds?

Children in that age range do not have the ability to comprehend or manipulate concepts as you do. There is no vocabulary that can communicate sophisticated ideas as clearly to them as those ideas can be communicated to adults. To teach children, you must model what you want to teach. If you want to teach them not to judge other people, you must stop judging other people yourself.

A mother once brought her little girl to Gandhi and asked him, "Will you tell my girl not to eat sugar?"

"Bring her back in three weeks," said Gandhi. When the mother returned with the girl in three weeks, Gandhi told the girl gently, "Don't eat sugar. It is not good for you."

"Why did you wait three weeks to tell her that?" asked the mother.

"Because," said Gandhi, "three weeks ago I was eating sugar!"

When you learn to teach this way, with your example as well as your words, you will be much more effective with everyone, and especially with children.

HOW DO I MOVE MY CHILDREN TOWARD AUTHENTIC POWER?
I am not sure where to start with my thirteen-year-old daughter.

The first step in moving your children toward authentic power is creating it in your life. Emotional awareness—becoming aware of everything that you are feeling all of the time—is not modeled in schools, among teen peers, or in families. Developing emotional awareness is difficult because it requires you to look clearly at your obsessions, compulsions, and addictions, and to experience the painful physical sensations that lie beneath them. These are the origins of your repetitive dysfunctions. They are the cause of your emotional flare-ups or the fearful distance that you keep from your children. Until you develop this ability, or begin the process of developing it, you will not be able to demonstrate, or even explain, its value to your children. Without developing emotional awareness, creating authentic power is not possible for you or for your children.

You must develop the ability to make responsible choices. A responsible choice is a choice that creates consequences for which you are willing to assume responsibility. Teenagers, in particular, are sensitive to issues of responsibility because they are often used to manipulate them into behaviors they do not value or want. When parents say, for example, "Be a man." "When are you going to grow up?" or "When I was your age . . ." they create resistance to the idea of responsibility because that idea becomes identified in the experience of the teenager with manipulation. This identification is accurate.

Responsible choice requires you to come to terms with your creative powers and the reality of the consequences that they create in your life. If you can choose to speak without anger while you are feeling enraged, or to reach out to your child while you are feeling rejected or inferior, your actions model clarity and courage. If you lose your temper, shout, emotionally withdraw, and in other ways attempt to manipulate and control your children, you model the pursuit of external power—the ability to manipulate and control those things that appear to be external, including other people.

Your intuition is continually providing you with inspiration, insight, hunches, and information that you can use as you interact with others, including your children. Ask yourself, "If I were wise and compassionate, how would I handle this situation?" and listen for an answer. If you are about to say or do something that you are not sure you want to say or do, ask yourself, "What is my motivation?" You will not be alone in your assessment. If your intention is to make yourself feel safe, lovable, or worthy by dominating a child, or attempting to, you will see that and be able to change it. If you ignore your intuition, you set the example of not drawing upon the wisdom and compassion that is available to you, or choosing not to listen to it.

Trust is the most challenging of all the components of authentic power, and also the most healing. It lightens your load. When you doubt your ability to parent well, to live well, or to contribute to Life, remind yourself that each of your experiences is perfect for you, given the wisdom of the choices that you have made. Remind yourself that the Universe is alive, wise, and compassionate, and that an intelligence beyond your own is working toward your benefit and the benefit of your child in each interaction.

HOW CAN I SET AN EXAMPLE FOR OTHERS?

Is it possible to set an example for someone else without expecting a particular reaction or response?

Yes. Here is how you can do it:

1. Consult your intuition. Ask for guidance and open to it. Listen for it. Allow your insights and inspiration to come in the ways that they will, even if that is not how you think they should come.

2. Set your intention before you interact. Know what you want to accomplish. For example, is your intention to come closer, or to influence or control? If it is to influence or control, pick another intention.

3. Speak from your heart. In other words, don't intellectualize, theorize, or hypothesize, but share what is important to you in a personal and considerate way.

4. Detach from the outcome. If you are disappointed or angry at the outcome, you had a second agenda, and that agenda was to manipulate and control.

5. Try again.

6. Enjoy yourself.

Physical and Spiritual Health

WHAT IS A HEALTHY DIET?

What constitutes for you a cleansing, healing diet? How can it help?

Healthy meals will not create authentic power for you. They will facilitate your intention to look inside yourself honestly and with courage. They will support your intentions to create authentic power, but they are not a substitute for the work that you must do. Some foods have higher vibrations than others, which means more energy than others. Eating foods with high vibrations does not mean you are on the road to enlightenment and not eating them does not mean that you are not. As you strive for emotional and physical health, your diet can support your efforts but it won't replace them. If you only eat broccoli and tofu, for example, but you are filled with judgments or seething with rage, you might as well eat roast beef.

Cooked food has a lower vibration than raw food. Food with artificially added chemicals has a lower vibration than food without them. Artificial colors, artificial flavors, most preservatives, and genetically modified food are not healthy. You were not designed to eat them and they were not designed with your health in mind. Vegetables have higher vibrations than meats, and meats with altered genetic codes, growth hormones, and antibiotics are bad for your health. Most meat has all of these. Most dairy products have them, too.

Uncooked organic vegetables have the most energy, and highly cooked, highly processed foods with added chemicals have the least. Even so, an all-vegetable diet may not be appropriate for you. Take your time. Listen to what your body wants. That will show you your addictions—to caffeine, to sugar, to nicotine—and also show you what gives you energy and strength.

Over twenty years ago I shifted from a meat and frozen-food diet to an all-vegetarian diet because I was copying a friend who ate more consciously than I did. It didn't feel good, or satisfying, and it didn't last long. Now, at home, Linda and I eat mostly organic vegetables, organic fruit, organic chicken, and fish. We do the best we can when we travel.

However, food is not the only thing that you eat. When you think of a healthy diet, consider your thoughts also. What vibrational level are they? Are you judging your neighbors or coworkers? Are you working hard to win something someone else wants, such as a trophy or a stock option to make you feel superior to others? These thoughts are toxins. How many are you eating? Are you content? That is a high vibrational state, and so are thoughts that accompany contentment. Are you filled with meaning and purpose? That is a very high vibrational state. Do you feel love for everyone around you? That is the highest vibrational state.

As you begin to lighten your energy—by challenging your anger, fear, jealousy, and anxieties—you will naturally become attracted to food that is lighter, also. As this happens, treat yourself kindly.

Kindness is healthy, too.

WHAT IS THE ROLE OF FITNESS AND PHYSICAL HEALTH?

People spend hours at gyms, eat special diets, and are obsessed with fitness and health. How connected or disconnected is this to our spiritual health?

Physical health and spiritual health are not the same. I was most healthy physically when I was least healthy spiritually. I ran thirty miles a week and disdained those who couldn't. I ate vegetarian food and disdained those who didn't. My pulse, blood pressure, endurance, and strength were maximal. My awareness of the beauty and purpose of my life was minimal.

I never realized the connection between the back spasms that crippled me and my anger. I even became angry with the spasms. I never appreciated my body, even though it was lean and beautiful. I didn't think of myself, including my body, as beautiful. I didn't like myself and I didn't like other people, either. I was resentful and depressed. Running and physical fitness kept me from feeling these things—sometimes.

I ran because that was part of my identity. It was a way that I felt superior, and attractive, especially to women. While my body was finely tuned, my spiritual growth was stagnant. It remained that way while I was obsessed with impressing others. That is the root obsession. The fixation is not on health but on anesthetizing a terrifying sense of powerlessness. It is a thirst for appreciation, even for a moment. It is a way of asking for love.

When you are a fountain of love, you do not need to ask for it. You are a source of it. Then your impulse to have a vital body is a natural expression of inner health. It is natural to run for the pleasure of it, to dance, and to walk in the sun. It is natural to breathe deeply, stretch fully, and move through your life with a limber body and a limber mind.

As you move through the stages of your life, honor your body. Illness is a major learning experience in the Earth school. Everyone experiences it. Everyone also dies. Do what you can to maintain a vital and healthy body. Physical matter is the densest projection of spiritual matter, but it is holy and it needs to be honored. Your body is an instrument that you will utilize until you die. Why not keep it vital?

Spiritual growth requires an open heart, looking past your defenses and beyond, and caring for people. You can create these things in a hospital bed or running by the ocean. What is appropriate and natural for you will emerge with your awareness of yourself as a powerful and creative, loving and compassionate spirit.

WHAT IS THE RELATION OF DIET AND SPIRITUALITY?

I have been a vegetarian for fifteen years and all of a sudden have depleted my B$_{12}$ and iron levels and have to eat meat. How does that relate to my spiritual journey?

Your spiritual journey requires that you become emotionally aware, learn to make responsible choices, and use that ability to align your personality with your soul. This journey is often as difficult as it is rewarding. It is always good to cultivate a vital, healthy body. Eating organic, fresh foods is one way to ensure that you do not eat preservative chemicals or radiated or genetically modified foods.

Meat is a more complex food than uncooked vegetables, but eating it does not mean that you are not on a spiritual journey. Many people refuse to eat meat, yet they daily ingest their judgments of others, critical thoughts, anger, resentment, jealousy, and fear. These are poisons. Why eat pure foods when nothing else you ingest is healthy? Many people who eat meat have a relationship with Life that is reverent and that respects the natural exchange of energy between the domains of Life on the Earth—mineral, vegetable, animal, and human.

Your intentions determine the trajectory of your life. If you are not aware of them, you follow a path that may lead you to places that you do not want to go. When you become aware of your emotions, learn to make responsible choices, and strive to create with the intentions of your soul, you encounter every part of your personality that opposes those intentions and are given the opportunity to challenge and change them. Your body will tell you what it needs. Your job is to develop the ability to listen—not to follow your compulsions or the unexamined advice of others.

ARE ANTIDEPRESSANTS USEFUL?

Are antidepressants a valuable tool in fighting depression, or do they just mask the work that I need to do in order to create authentic power?

Depression is a complex phenomenon. It is the surface manifestation of a deep, multilayered dynamic. Depression is painful beyond what those who have not experienced it can imagine, yet it covers even more painful experiences that need to be unearthed and healed. Anger is one of those experiences. Beneath anger lies fear, and at the root of depression lies lack of self-value. Lack of self-value, or the experience of powerlessness, is the core of all painful human experiences and destructive actions.

Antidepressants cannot reach these dynamics that lie beneath your depression and fuel it, yet they can provide a respite that you can use wisely. Like grace, which temporarily allows you to see what your life would be like if you lived to your highest potential in the moment, antidepressants provide you with temporary relief from the pain of your depression and allow you to see what your life could be like without your depression.

If you use the brief times that antidepressants provide to look deeply into your life, they will be an aid to you. If you use them to return to the same unexamined life that created your depression, they will be a crutch that you will find increasingly undependable. No matter how much pain your antidepressant masks, the consequences of that pain will continue to create the same misery that clinicians called a depression.

Chemical imbalance always accompanies emotional distress but does not cause it. Chemical imbalance is a correlate of that distress. This correlation is what allows antidepressants to alter your emotional experience in the moment without changing what causes it. Changing what causes it is your job. Your depression, like every painful emotion, brings your attention to what needs to be changed in you, by you.

Messages from
Your Soul

WHAT IS THE MEANING OF DREAMS?

What do dreams have to do with my life? Are they a tool for discovery, and how can they be used?

Dreams are comments on your life. They are valuable perspectives that are meant to inform you of what you need to consider at the moment. If you were to receive letters daily that provided you information that could change your life, would you open them? Would you take the time to read them, even if the handwriting were difficult to decipher?

Dreams are your nightly letters. They are messages from your soul. They are not meant to scare you, even if that is how you feel after or during a dream. They are meant to tell you something that is important for you to know about yourself at that moment in your life. This is different from dream interpretation. Dream interpretation is an approach to understanding dreams that served five-sensory humans—individuals who were limited in their perception to the five senses. It has helped numerous individuals understand more about themselves and the collectives of which they are a part.

Understanding dreams as messages from the soul is a multi-sensory approach to dreams. Dream interpretation is seeing dreams from the outside in. Understanding dreams as messages from the soul is understanding them from the inside out. That is significantly different.

If you do not understand the message your soul is bringing to you, your next dream the same night will repeat the message, and the next, throughout the night. In other words, if you write your dreams during the night but do not consider them until the morning, when you wake you will have a collection of dream experiences, each conveying the same meaning. That meaning has to do with you and your life.

You will receive more letters the next night, and the next for the duration of your time in the Earth school. Each one brings you new messages, the latest-breaking, most up-to-date news available in a special edition prepared just for you. How you use these special-edition communications from your soul is up to you.

WHAT IS THE ROLE OF MY SOUL IN MY LIFE?

What does my soul have to do with my life?

The question is not, "What is the role of your soul in your life?" The question is, "What is the role of your life in your soul?" You are an energy tool of your soul. You were born on one date and you will die on another. Your soul is that part of you that existed before you were born and will continue to exist when you die. It is that part of you that is eternal. Your soul uses your personality, not the other way around. Your soul is immensely larger than you. Its comprehension is immensely larger and its compassion is immensely larger. Its experience is different.

Anger, jealousy, resentment, anxiety, and the many other forms of fear are experiences of the Earth school. They reflect in the domain of the five senses those parts of your soul that your soul desires to heal. That healing comes with your decisions to respond consciously and compassionately to the challenges of your life. That is your job. When you use your intentions—the force of your will—to align your personality with your soul, you create authentic power. You become humble, forgiving, clear, and loving. You treasure Life. You are happy to be on the Earth, even in your most difficult moments.

Your life is an opportunity to do these things. It is also your opportunity to give the gifts that your soul wants to give. You cannot do that while you are in the grip of anger, jealousy, sorrow, or fear. You cannot enjoy the fulfillment of a life lived consciously and meaningfully. Your time on the Earth is the opportunity to create such a life—to use your will intelligently, wisely, and compassionately. When you do, you become a conduit for the energy of your soul. What your soul wants, you want. What your soul treasures, you treasure.

Learning how to create what your soul treasures moment by moment is the role of your life in your soul.

WHY ARE SOULS CREATED IMPERFECT?

If souls have parts of themselves that need healing, doesn't that mean that they are wounded, or not whole?

Everything in the Universe moves toward ever-increasing awareness and freedom. Everything in the Universe, including you, your soul, everyone else, and every soul, participates in a continual unfolding of potential. This is evolution. If you think that perfection is already here, look around and see if you can find anyone who is perfect. You will not. Every personality in the Earth school has lessons to learn and gifts to give that have not yet been given. Every soul, also, participates in the continual movement toward fuller and fuller expression of wisdom and compassion. That movement is what created you, and all that you do offers you the opportunity to contribute to it.

At the same time, if you could see clearly, you would see that each experience is perfectly suited to the individual who encounters it, given the wisdom of the choices that he or she has made. Every circumstance serves equally the evolution of all involved, offering each individual the perfect opportunity to create anew and, hopefully, create more wisely and compassionately. No individual in the Earth school is perfect, yet the process in which all individuals participate is worthy and perfect.

Your soul is not a perfected ideal, like the philosopher Plato described. It evolves and the process of its evolution is perfect. Do not concern yourself with seeking perfection or longing for a perfect soul. The Universe is perfect, and you are a perfect part of the Universe. You cannot change that. You can only choose what you will contribute and, therefore, experience as you and the Universe evolve. If you choose cruelty, self-interest, and exploitation, the consequences of your choices—violence and destruction—will appear perfectly in your life, offering you opportunities to grow into greater freedom and awareness. If you choose kindness, care for others and contribution to Life, the consequences of your choices—contentment and wholeness—will appear perfectly in your life, offering you opportunities to grow into greater freedom and awareness.

All roads lead to home.

IS IT POSSIBLE TO EXPERIENCE MY SOUL?

How can I feel my soul?

When your life fills with meaning, you experience your soul. You are on the path that your soul wants to take. When your life is devoid of meaning, you experience your soul. You are on a path that your soul does not want to take.

When you experience your emotions, you feel your soul. Your emotions are the force field of your soul. Painful emotions, such as anger, jealousy, resentment, and vengefulness are expressions of fear. They are the parts of your personality that your soul wants to bring into wholeness. These parts reflect in the experience of your personality the parts of your soul that your soul wants to heal. Your soul does not experience anger, jealousy, resentment, and vengefulness. It experiences distance from Light—uncontaminated conscious Love. You experience that as a form of fear.

When you use your intuition, you sometimes experience your soul. Intuition is the voice of the nonphysical world. Through your intuition you access information that is not available to you through the five senses. Sometimes this information comes from nonphysical guides and nonphysical Teachers. Sometimes it comes from fellow souls. Sometimes it comes from your own soul. This is the higher-self experience.

Your soul is at the center of all that you experience. It is your essence. It is the part of you that is immortal. It is a powerful presence. As you align your personality with your soul, you become powerful, too. Your life becomes more and more joyful, no matter what is occurring in it—even events that others would consider tragic. That, also, is an experience of your soul.

WHY DO SOULS LEAVE WHEN THEY STILL HAVE WORK TO DO?

I don't think my dad's soul had finished what it was supposed to do when he died at the young age of fifty-three. Can you explain why souls leave when they still have so much to do?

A soul leaves the Earth school when it is ready to leave the Earth school. It is your perception that the soul of your father had more to do in the Earth school, but that was not the perception of your father's soul or it would not have left. When a soul decides to go home—to return to nonphysical reality—nothing can stop it. Until then, nothing can make it return home. There is perfection in each experience, and your father's departure from the Earth school is part of it.

WHAT IS THE DIFFERENCE BETWEEN A PERSONALITY AND A SOUL?

Please explain the difference between a soul and a personality.

Your personality is that part of you that was born on a certain date and will die on a certain date. Your soul is that part of you that existed before you were born and that will continue to exist after you die. Your personality is that part of you that is mortal. Your soul is that part of you that is immortal.

When you look at yourself as a personality, you think of yourself as a body and a mind. When you look at yourself as a soul, you think of yourself as a powerful and creative, compassionate and loving spirit that has entered the Earth school in order to learn lessons and to give gifts.

Your personality is a tool of your soul. It is a part of your soul that is on a mission. It has all of the power of your soul, but that power is calibrated to a certain set of circumstances. Those circumstances are the experiences of the five senses.

Your personality is a complex pattern of parts of your soul that your soul desires to heal and parts of your soul that your soul has lent to your personality for its journey through the Earth school. The parts of your personality that your soul desires to heal are the parts of yourself that are angry, jealous, vengeful, self-righteous, feeling superior, feeling inferior, and more. They are the frightened parts. The parts of your personality that your soul has lent to it for its journey through the Earth school are the parts of you that are generous, gracious, kind, patient, grateful, caring, and compassionate. They are the loving parts.

The purpose of a journey in the Earth school is to discover the frightened parts of your personality and heal them, and to discover the loving parts of your personality and cultivate them. If you do not do this, your soul creates another personality for another journey through the Earth school.

As you become multisensory, you begin to see yourself as a soul first and a personality second. You begin to experience yourself as more than a body and a mind and the circumstances around you as meaningful and designed for your spiritual growth—even those that are painful.

As long as you live on the Earth you will have a personality—a body, a mind, and a way of experiencing intuition. When your personality dies, your soul returns to its home. Its home is nonphysical reality.

HOW DO I KEEP FROM FEELING AT CONSTANT ODDS WITH MY PERSONALITY?

My personality keeps generating emotions like resentment, anger, etc. How do I keep from feeling antagonistic toward my personality?

Your personality is an energy tool that your soul has adapted in order to learn through the experience of physicalness. It is your body, intuitional structure (the way that you experience intuition), and what psychology defines as a "personality"—your cognition (how you think), perception (how you see things), and affect (your emotions). As long as you are alive, you will have a personality. Being in the Earth school and having a personality are the same thing.

The painful experiences that you encounter, such as resentment, anger, and vengefulness, are the parts of your personality that your soul desires to heal. They are the parts of your personality that are not aligned with your soul. Your soul wants to create harmony, sharing, cooperation, and reverence for Life. These parts of your personality do not.

Your painful experiences are signposts that point directly to parts of your personality that need healing. When you feel resentment, anger, or other painful emotions, it is because you have encountered a part of your personality that is not integrated and whole. Becoming integrated and whole is the spiritual path. Your personality is your vehicle.

Your job is not to become angry or dissatisfied with your personality. It is to learn about yourself from your experiences and change yourself rather than continue to have the same painful experiences again and again. That is spiritual growth.

CAN SOULS COMMUNICATE WITH US AFTER THEIR PERSONALITIES DIE?

Do you believe in psychics or people who can communicate with souls after the death of a person's physical body?

This is not a matter of belief. As individuals become multisensory, their perceptual capabilities expand beyond the limitations of the five senses and such communication becomes possible. This is now happening in millions of individuals. All of us will soon become multisensory. Your soul did not come into being when you were born and it will not cease to exist when you die. The same is true for each human. Our fundamental relationship is soul to soul. As we become multisensory, we become aware of that.

Nonphysical Reality

DO WE NEED TO GROW INTO "GREAT SOULS"?

Do we need to grow into "great souls" before we have the chance of leaving the Earth school?

Each individual is a personality in a soul. A soul is more expansive, compassionate, and wiser than its personality can experience. You do not need to become a "great soul" in order to leave the Earth school. You will leave the Earth school when you die. When you return home to nonphysical reality you reenter the fullness of your soul.

There is greatness in every personality that lives the intentions of its soul. It develops humbleness, clarity, forgiveness, and love. This is the creation of authentic power—the alignment of the personality with the soul. Creating authentic power is your evolutionary pathway. You cannot evolve without creating it, and you cannot create it without inner work. As you become authentically powerful, your life becomes "great." Nobility replaces pettiness, compassion replaces cruelty, and appreciation of Life replaces exploitation of Life.

Some souls have influence over a few individuals, while others have influence over many more. Some have influence over millions of individuals. The more influence a personality acquires over others, the more responsibility it assumes, and the more nonphysical guidance becomes available to it. Whether that guidance is utilized is a matter of choice. We say that a personality that uses its influence to create harmony where there was discord, sharing where there was hoarding, cooperation where there was competition, and contribution to Life where there was exploitation of Life is great. This greatness does not depend upon the number of individuals who are influenced by it, but by the way it chooses to use its influence.

You do not need to be the president of a nation or a television celebrity to live a life of greatness. You embark upon that course when you begin the pursuit of authentic power. You do not need to live a life of greatness in order to leave the Earth school. Your exit from the Earth school is assured no matter what you choose while you are in it.

WHAT IS INTUITION?

How do I find my intuition or inner voice?

The entire human family is expanding beyond the limitations of the five senses—taste, touch, sight, hearing, and smell. That means, among other things, it is becoming able to access information the five senses cannot provide. That is intuition.

Intuition is the voice of the nonphysical world. As you become multisensory, you become intuitive. You do not need to find your intuition. It will find you. Each individual experiences intuition in a different way. Some hear voices. Some hear sounds and others see colors. Some people feel sensations. There is no correct way to experience intuition. Your intuitional structure—the way you experience intuition—is as unique as your body.

Multisensory perception is also the ability to see meaning in everyday circumstances. You may see, for example, how perfect an experience is for you, or for someone else. All of your experiences are perfect for you given the wisdom of the choices you have made. Multisensory perception is seeing that.

You have nonphysical guides and Teachers. You access them through your intuition. You "hear" them through your insights, inspirations, and clarity. Nonphysical Teachers cannot control you. You must always decide for yourself how you will use your energy—what you will create. They will assist you to see your choices and the consequences of each. They will guide you to the full scope and depth of your power. How you choose to use your power is up to you.

Multisensory perception is very different from your imagination and your intellect. Your intellect will rationalize what you want to do. Your intuition will surprise you. Be gentle with yourself as you experiment with your intuition. Do not too quickly dismiss the ideas that you are no longer limited to the perceptions of the five senses, that your life is meaningful, and that you have nonphysical assistance.

HOW DOES INTUITION DIFFER FROM PARANOIA?

I find it difficult to determine the difference between intuition and paranoia. Can you help?

Intuition is the voice of the nonphysical world. It broadens your perception and understanding. It assists you in making choices that are in alignment with the highest parts of your personality. It serves your survival, creativity, and spiritual growth. It is a blessing that enables you to move more fully into your own power and authority. It provides you ways to grow in wholeness, deepen in compassion, and expand in wisdom.

Paranoia contracts your consciousness. It focuses your attention on circumstances that are external to you. It is magnetic and compulsive. It satisfies the most insecure parts of your personality, separates you from others, and is painful.

Intuition offers you choices. Paranoia imposes choices upon you. Intuition shows you avenues to health. Paranoia deprives you of health. Intuition will often surprise you by suggesting what you have not thought about, or challenging what you think you want to do. Paranoia will rationalize what you want to do.

Intuition is a conduit to the wisdom and compassion of nonphysical guides and Teachers. Their only interest is your spiritual growth. Paranoia is the voice of the parts of your personality that are most frightened. They fear most what your intuition seeks to show you.

If you are confused about whether you are experiencing intuition or paranoia, ask yourself these questions: "Will what

I am considering create harmony? Will it create sharing? Will it create cooperation? Does it revere Life?" These are the critical questions of the soul. When you are in touch with your intuition, the answers will always be yes.

Addiction and Healing

WHAT IS THE DIFFERENCE BETWEEN HABIT AND ADDICTION?

I have habits but I am not sure I have any addictions. What is the difference?

A habit is a repetitive behavior that masks uncomfortable feelings from you. For example, you may have the habit of drinking coffee each morning, watching TV in the evening, wearing certain clothes on Tuesdays, etc. These behaviors cover stress or anxiety. It is easy to verify this for yourself. If you intentionally do not do these behaviors, you begin to feel anxious or uncomfortable. Among many other habits that you may use to hide your uncomfortable emotions from you are workaholism—continually working until you are exhausted—and perfectionism—the need to keep your office or home in a particular order. Behaviors such as these are even more difficult to change because when you don't do them you feel very uncomfortable. For example, if you stop working you very soon feel an intense need to start again, or when you leave your desk in disarray you will feel very uneasy until you put it in order again.

Addictions are also behaviors that mask emotions, but those emotions are so painful that instead of experiencing them you feel an irresistible urge to do something, such as shop, smoke, gamble, take a drug, watch pornography, drink alcohol, or have sex. You crave the behavior that you do not have. In other words, all unconscious behaviors, including addictions, mask painful emotions, but an addiction is a habit that masks emotions that are so painful that your need to avoid them is so great that you feel you *must* engage in the behavior. You do not think in terms of avoiding painful emotions. Instead you feel an overpowering, irresistible attraction—to sex, alcohol, a cigarette, etc.

Changing unconscious behaviors requires becoming aware of what lies beneath them, and that requires developing emotional awareness.

HOW CAN I OVERCOME MY ADDICTION?

If I have an addiction, how do I take away its power?

Your addictions are your greatest inadequacies. They are the parts of your personality that are out of your control, which means they are the parts of yourself that are most controlled by external circumstances.

Healing your addictions is a sacred task, and it is the task that you were born to accomplish. Locating, acknowledging, and challenging your greatest inadequacies is the heart of the spiritual path because your spiritual growth—your ability to move beyond these limiting parts of your personality—is directly at issue. Healing an addiction is a complex matter, but the important thing to remember is that your addiction is not stronger than who you want to become.

The first step in healing an addiction is to acknowledge that you have it. Until you do, you will not acknowledge that a part of yourself is out of control, but once you have seen that a part of yourself is out of control, you must choose to leave it out of your control or do something about it. Your intention to heal your addictions is a necessary and deeply significant step in your spiritual development.

WHAT IS THE REASON FOR STRUGGLES AND ADDICTIONS?

I have just celebrated my one-year AA anniversary but I fought and struggled with drug addiction for twenty-eight years. A reason?

I am not a therapist or one who knows much about your life, but one thing is clear to me. If you have been addicted to drugs for twenty-eight years and you have now celebrated one year of sobriety, you have strengths and insights that you could not have imagined during the time that you were addicted.

Healing an addiction is the deepest spiritual work that you can do. It is not possible to heal an addiction without the courage to face parts of your personality that are out of control and to discover their roots. It requires seeing with clarity the ugliness that you once found so attractive.

Each individual uncovers different things about himself or herself on this difficult journey, but everyone who takes it emerges transformed from an individual who flees the present moment into one who lives in the present moment gratefully. The healing of an addiction is the beginning of a story, not the end of one. It enables the expansion of your consciousness and your life into their fuller capability and purpose. It frees your awareness into its higher potential. What you do with your expanded capability and awareness is your choice, just as your decision to challenge and heal your addiction was your choice, and your continuing decisions to remain sober and grow healthy are your choices.

Look at who you are now, and ask yourself if you still need a reason for your addictive experiences.

CAN INVOLUNTARY BEHAVIOR BE CHANGED?

How do I change a behavior I want to change when the decision to act that way feels involuntary?

All of the behaviors that most need to be changed feel involuntary. They are your obsessions, compulsions, and, strongest of all, your addictions. These are the parts of your personality that are out of control. When you hear words that you do not want to hear, for example, and you are suddenly enraged, or withdrawn, you have encountered a part of your personality that is controlled by external circumstances.

If you see an open bottle of alcohol and you cannot resist taking a drink, or you find a willing sexual partner and you cannot resist engaging in sex, you have encountered a part of your personality that is out of control. Every painful emotion, and the reactions that they create in you feel involuntary. That is because they originate in parts of your personality that are operating outside the field of your awareness. In psychology, these parts are called the unconscious parts of your personality, although each one has its own consciousness—its own agenda, values, and perceptions. They are said to be "unconscious" because you are not aware of them until they become active, and you suddenly find yourself irritated, angry, jealous, vengeful, or frightened.

It is difficult to approach these parts of your personality because it is often shameful, and always painful, to do so. No one likes admitting that he or she is prejudiced, for example, yet most people have parts of their personality that are. Until those parts are acknowledged and healed, prejudice will be a part of their lives no matter how much they might detest prejudices of any kind.

The behaviors in yourself that appear to you to be involuntary are the places to start your spiritual journey. They are the flags that tell you that you have inner work to do. That inner work begins with feeling all that you are feeling the next time you encounter an involuntary behavior. When you do, you will discover that much of what you are feeling is painful. The first step in creating authentic power in your life is to begin to experience the painful emotions that torment you without trying to make them disappear by reaching outward to manipulate and control the circumstances around you—by shouting at someone, for example, or drinking, eating, having sex, buying something new, or any of the many ways that you have used in the past to make yourself feel better, safe, and lovable.

As you become aware of the unconscious parts of your personality and begin to challenge them you will find that, although their power is strong, the behaviors that they desire are not involuntary. The more you challenge them, the more they lose power over you. Eventually their power over you disintegrates.

That is how to change an involuntary behavior. It is also how to create authentic power.

HOW LONG WILL IT TAKE TO FIND ALL OF THE UNHEALED PARTS OF MYSELF?

I had done a lot of work to heal, enhanced my spiritual life, become a deeper thinking person, and started to pray. Then BOOM, I discover that I am addicted to something. When does this madness stop?

Discovering parts of your personality that are out of control is not the madness. It is part of the process of ending the madness. Until you are able to locate within yourself the sources of your uncontrollable attractions—to sex, alcohol, drugs, shopping, gambling, or anything else—you will continue to be out of control.

Acknowledging an obsession, compulsion, and, in particular, an addiction puts you in a position to do something about it. Then the work can begin. Healing your obsessions, compulsions, and addictions is the work that you were born to do. They stand between you and the life that your soul desires. You cannot create what your soul wants to create while you are obsessed, compelled, or addicted.

The process of unearthing unconscious parts of your personality does not last forever. Do not be discouraged by what you find or how long it takes. Celebrate that you are on the path, at last, toward wholeness.

WHAT IS MY RESPONSIBILITY TO FRIENDS AND FAMILY MEMBERS WHO ARE ADDICTED OR IN EMOTIONAL PAIN?

What is my responsibility to someone close to me who is addicted or in deep emotional pain?

Your responsibility to friends and family members who are addicts is to remain balanced and centered and to continue your own spiritual growth. When you encounter an individual who is addicted or in intense emotional pain, you encounter at the same time a reality that is real and forceful for that individual yet is not the reality that you experience. The addict, who is always in emotional pain, will attempt to convince you, blame you, reason with you, shout at you, or control you in any way he can into accepting his painful emotional reality. If you accept his blame, reasoning, or control, you engage in what the recovery community calls "enabling." You assist your friend in the continuation of his addiction or the prolongation of his pain.

His addiction and pain are real. They are designed to bring to his attention parts of his personality that he needs to examine and change, yet his words and behavior are all focused on the opposite—avoiding exploration of the causes of his addiction and emotional pain. That exploration begins with the idea of self-responsibility—entertaining the possibility that he has created what he is experiencing. This idea frequently causes explosive denial on the part of the addict or emotionally distressed individual. That is where your balance and clarity are needed.

Understanding Karma

WHY DO I GET SUCH BAD KARMA?

I think I am a good person yet the universe treats me badly. I work hard and yet I don't get anything I want. I do not understand why I am getting such bad Karma.

Karma is neither good nor bad. Karma is the experience of what you have created. It is the compassionate dynamic through which you learn to create responsibly. Karma is the law of cause and effect through which you shape your life with every decision. There are no good effects or bad effects. There are only effects. You choose the cause and that choice is also the choice of an effect. The cause and the effect are one. Neither can exist without the other. If you participate in the cause, you will always participate in its effect, also. There are no exceptions.

You feel that the Universe is treating you badly, but it is not. It is treating you the way you have asked it to treat you. You tell the Universe how to treat you when you make choices. When you create suffering, you experience suffering. When you create joy, you experience joy. Sooner or later, you will make the connection between what you choose and what you experience. Then you will choose differently.

Karma draws your attention to what you have created. Is your attention not captured when you are in pain? Asking why the Universe is treating you badly when you experience painful circumstances in your life is like asking a mirror why you look the way that you do. Your reflection will not change until you change. Karma is your reflection. You can throw away a mirror, but your reflection will be the same when you look into another one. You can blame the Universe for your pain, but your pain will continue. Only you can change that and, eventually, you will.

CAN VISUALIZATION AND AFFIRMATION CHANGE KARMA?

Can visualization and affirmation counter the effects of Karma? Are they in vain if they are contrary to the Karma that I must experience?

You experience what you create. That is Karma. Not even your nonphysical Teachers can change that. Nothing can. You are responsible for how you choose to use your energy. All else is wishful thinking. The Universe is wise and compassionate. Experiencing what you create is the Universe's gracious way of assisting you in developing the ability to create consciously. How else could you learn to wield your power compassionately and wisely in all circumstances, at all times? That is what you were born to learn, and Karma is the tool that teaches you thoroughly and irrevocably. Once you experience a pain that you have created in another person and recognize what you have done, you will not do that again.

Affirmations and visualizations are ways of focusing intention. Intentions cannot prevent you from encountering what you have created. Each encounter with what you have created is a lesson to be learned. You are the vehicle for this educational process. However, your intentions can alter the way you experience the consequences that you have created. For example, if you intend to see the circumstances of your life as the unfolding of Karma, you will not be so quick to blame others for what you experience. You will be able to detach from your experiences in ways that you would not otherwise. You will not take things so personally. This will allow you to respond in ways that create Karma that is not painful. When you see the people in your life with gratitude instead of resentment, you will not harm them or want to.

When you set the intention to respond compassionately to everything that you experience, you also allow your Karma to open your heart rather than close it. When you hold the intention to see yourself as a student in the Earth school, you utilize your experiences as they were intended to be used—to expand your awareness of yourself as a powerful creator, and your freedom to create consciously.

Karma is a gift from the Universe. It is a gift that you cannot visualize or affirm away. As your awareness grows, it will become a gift that you cherish.

SHOULD I INTERFERE WITH SOMEONE'S KARMA?

If I watch as someone I love is being molested, do I simply say to myself, "That must be his/her Karma and I am not to judge or interfere"?

You cannot interfere with someone else's Karma. You can only make your own Karma. If you see an act of violence and you say to yourself, "He must deserve this, or it wouldn't be happening. His suffering is not my concern," what Karma are you creating? The indifference that you show to a fellow soul is the same indifference that you will encounter. Is this what you want?

An act of violence may not be as dramatic as a fight or a sexual assault. Indifference is a violent action. So is greed, jealousy, and every impulse to exploit another soul or the Earth. Do you want to give to Life? That desire is nurturing. Do you want to take from it? That impulse is violent.

If you decide that it is not your business when someone else suffers, don't think that your understanding of Karma will permit your act of callousness to go without its effects upon you. The suffering that you see is fair. Every experience in the Earth school is fair, but if you use your realization of this to ignore the suffering of your brothers and sisters, you create a world in which your suffering, also, is of no concern to others. That is Karma.

Your future is yours to create in the same way that you created your present—through your choices. Compassion or indifference is a choice. It is natural for us to be compassionate, but we can choose "not to get involved." Feeling warmly toward one another is natural for us, but we can choose to be distant and cold. Everything that you do is a choice and every choice that you make creates experiences that you will encounter. That is Karma.

Getting involved does not mean judging. You may feel righteously angry at a sexual molester, but beware if you do. You do not know enough to judge—this act or any other. You do not know what is being healed, or coming to completion. Molester and molested may be exchanging roles that were played in another lifetime. It is not your role to be a judge or a jury. If you decide to take on these roles, you create painful Karma for yourself. Do you like being judged?

Doing what you can to protect the molested from the molester is appropriate. Judging the molester is not. Protecting the bullied and the oppressed is appropriate. Judging the bully and the oppressor is not. Do you have the courage to protect without judging? Can you be compassionate even to those who have no compassion? If so, there is no finer Karma that you can create. You will live in a world that is compassionate with you, even when you forget to be compassionate. You will be supported when you are weak until you have regained your strength. You will be loved, even if you forget to love.

How would you like to create that?

WILL I CREATE NEGATIVE KARMA BY TAKING A JOB IN A COMPANY THAT SUPPORTS PEOPLE'S ADDICTIONS?

I'm about to take a job that will challenge me and give me new skills, but this company has practices that are in conflict with my belief system. Will I create negative Karma by participating in something that contributes to others' addictions?

You create Karma whenever you make a choice. Every choice you make is a cause and every cause has an effect. When you encounter the effects that you have caused, that is your Karma. Your moment-to-moment experience is a series of consequences that you have created, and your response to what each moment brings to you creates more effects—more Karma.

Effects are neither positive nor negative. They are consequences that your choice of causes create. If those consequences are wholesome and life-supporting, we call them positive. If they are painful and destructive, we call them negative. Those labels are ours. The Universe does not judge. It compassionately provides for us the consequences that we create with our choices, whatever those consequences are. That is how Karma works.

When you participate in a cause that brings suffering to others, you will participate also in the effects of that cause. That means you will encounter the same suffering in the intimacy of your own experience. This process is complex and exact. If you choose, for example, to take a job in an industry that thrives on the addictions of others, you draw to yourself people who will thrive on your inadequacies. As you choose to profit from the suffering of others, others will seek to profit from your suffering.

Is this the world that you desire? If so, take the job. The Universe will not judge you. Do you seek to create another world? Pay attention to your choices, choose wisely, and you will create another world. The Universe will not judge you in that case, either. The power to create your experience is fully in your hands. That is the lesson of Karma.

Challenge and Change

HOW DO I "CHALLENGE" MY ANGER OR FEAR?

How exactly do I challenge my fears, anger, and jealousy?

The first step in challenging a painful emotion is to become aware of it. Once you recognize how your body feels and the types of thoughts you have when it is present, you will no longer need to label it "anger," "fear," "jealousy," or anything else. You will know it as an old familiar experience that you want to change. Then you can challenge it directly. The simplest way to do this is to say to yourself, "I challenge this. I will not have this energy in my energy system," and mean it.

The first time you challenge your anger, fear, or jealousy, it will not disappear. You must challenge it again and again. Eventually it will lose power over you and you will gain power over it. This is how you create authentic power—decision by decision. You cannot pray, meditate, or wish it into being. You must challenge the parts of your personality that you want to change and cultivate the parts that you want to strengthen. This requires the use of your will.

If you do not challenge your anger, fear, or jealousy, you will die with it. Growing older does not automatically mean growing kinder or wiser. Millions of people die angry, frightened, and jealous. Unless you heal the parts of your personality that are causing you pain, they will not change. This is because no one can change them but you.

Putting yourself in the position of the other person challenges your anger. So does the intention to discover the pain that lies beneath your anger. Putting the needs of another above your own needs challenges your impatience. Looking for the miracles in your life challenges your depression. Every time you cultivate a part of your personality that you wish to keep, you challenge the parts of your personality that oppose it. You cannot be grateful and depressed at the same time. You cannot be angry and joyful at the same time. The choice is yours.

Do you cultivate your inner landscape, or do you give yourself reasons why you cannot be joyful, grateful, and optimistic? Cultivating a landscape takes time and effort, vision and perseverance.

Everyone has an inner landscape. Only you have the power to choose what grows in yours.

What is growing in yours now?

WHY DOES MY ANGER INCREASE WHEN I CHALLENGE IT?

I have been challenging my anger and now I feel overwhelmed by the amount of anger I have. I didn't realize how often angry thoughts run through my head. Is this progress?

Your anger does not disappear the first time you challenge it, or the second or the third. Gaining power over your anger requires you to challenge it again and again and yet again. Each time you challenge it, you gain power over it and it loses power over you. Eventually, its power over you disintegrates.

When you set the intention to heal your anger—or jealousy, anxiety, or any other fear—the Universe responds to your intention. The aspect of yourself that you challenge comes to the foreground of your consciousness. Everything begins to irritate. Friends say things that make you angry. Your dreams show you the archetypal roots of your anger. You have set the intention to heal your anger, and the Universe brings your anger up for you to challenge.

Your anger has not increased. Your awareness of it, and the number of opportunities that you have to challenge it, have increased. This is the gracious response of the Universe to your intention to heal. As you continue to challenge your anger, it begins to lose its power over you and you begin to gain power over it.

If you look at every recurrence of your anger as a setback, you do not recognize the compassion of the Universe or the power of your intention. The process of unearthing the unconscious parts of your personality is not endless. You are in the midst of a process that has a beginning, a middle, and an end. Challenging your anger is the beginning. Discovering the scope and depth of it is the middle.

That is progress.

WHAT IS THE DIFFERENCE BETWEEN CHALLENGING MY FEARS AND REPRESSING THEM?

When does challenging my emotions become repressing my emotions?

Never. It is not possible to repress an emotion and challenge it simultaneously. To challenge an emotion, you must first become aware of it. To challenge it effectively, you must come to know it very well. You must be able to recognize every aspect of it—where you feel it in your body, what kind of thoughts it creates, and what impulses it generates. You must be able to feel it coming and know how it affects you at the peak of its power. You must become intimate with it in every way. Only then will you be able to begin the process of coming to terms with it.

If someone appears in your life whenever he desires, creates confusion and painful consequences for you to deal with, and leaves as unexpectedly as he arrived, wouldn't you be on the lookout for him? Wouldn't you make a very serious effort to remember his face so that you could recognize him when he comes again, and pay attention to exactly what he does and how he does it? How could you challenge him in the future if you don't know how to recognize him, aren't sure of what he does, and your attention is focused on cleaning up after he leaves?

It is the same with your emotions. You must learn to recognize each of them that you desire to change and make the effort to learn everything about them that you can. That means paying close attention to your emotions and learning every detail about them. Then you will know exactly what you want to change about yourself.

Then you will also be able to make the changes in yourself that you want to make.

HOW CAN I REALLY CHANGE?

When I want to make a change in my life, be it big or small, are there any one or two things that I can do that will really commit me, or make the change effective?

Set the intention to change and hold it. Return to your intention often. It is better to renew an intention throughout the day rather than to set it once and assume that nothing more is required. The only change you will experience in your life is the change you choose to make. Only the intention to change yourself can change you, and you are the only one who can hold that intention.

HOW CAN I CHANGE MY UNCONSCIOUS INTENTIONS?

How do I change unconscious intentions that are sabotaging me?

You need to find within yourself all the parts of your personality that are not aligned with your soul. These are the frightened parts of your personality. They are the origin of your unconscious intentions.

The first step is to become aware of everything that you are feeling. Your emotions are the force field of your soul. You can't become a compassionate or caring person and be unaware of your emotions at the same time. Your emotions lead you directly to the parts of your personality that do not care about other people or the Earth. Finding those parts and acknowledging them is a fundamental step toward authentic power. There are other steps as well. Another is responsible choice. A responsible choice is a choice that creates consequences for which the chooser is willing to accept responsibility. Becoming aware of everything you're feeling enables you to make responsible choices. When you choose to create with the intentions of your soul, you activate all of the parts of your personality that prevent you from creating those things so that you can recognize them and heal them, one by one, choice by choice, decision by decision, as they arise.

WHY IS THE UNEXPECTED SO PAINFUL?

Why do I always get upset when things don't happen the way I thought they would?

The unexpected is the great teacher of flexibility, adaptability, and trust. It illuminates the distinction between expectations and intentions, between your emotional attachments and your preferences. When you are emotionally attached, you have expectations. When you have preferences, you have intentions that are independent of the outcome of your actions. The most emotionally charged attachment is almost always to the status quo, the familiar and predictable circumstances and events that give you the feeling that you know what will happen next, that you can depend upon for consistency. When this expectation is disrupted, when the status quo is disturbed or replaced altogether, the emotional reactions that are generated are always forceful and often cause great upset.

The status quo for each of us is continually being disrupted, and that is the source of our painful emotional experiences. When we resist change, we experience emotional pain and physical pain. When we welcome change, we relax and open to new possibilities. Resistance is an experience of fear and doubt, and openness is an experience of love and trust. When you resist, you fear that your needs will not be met and doubt that they ever will be. When you open to change, you love your life, embrace your experiences, no matter how difficult or pleasing, and trust that they are perfect for your spiritual growth.

The frequency and intensity of emotional reactions to the unexpected is an indicator of the degree of trust that is present or absent. The more intense and painful your reactions are, the less trust you have. When you have no fear, your trust is complete. Creating authentic power is the elimination of fear through emotional awareness, responsible choice, intuition, and the development of trust in the Universe. Your painful emotional reactions show you the frightened parts of your personality that you need to heal, your intentions allow you to respond instead of react, your intuition inspires and guides you, and your trust develops as you experience through your own efforts the joy of cocreating in partnership with the Universe, moment by moment, the most appropriate circumstances in space and time for your spiritual growth.

WHY DO NONPHYSICAL TEACHERS ALLOW VIOLENCE?

You say that nonphysical Teachers are all-knowing. As evidenced by what? Thousands of years of "civilized" society and THIS is as far as they've gotten us? And how compassionate can they be if they're lingering behind the scenes while Hitler kills six million Jews, blacks are confined to the back of the bus, and terrorists bomb whatever they can?

Nonphysical Teachers are impersonal energy dynamics. We personalize them, or think of them as having personalities like us, and sometimes we even give them names. Your nonphysical Teachers are not confined to the experiences of time, space, matter, and duality that characterize the Earth school, nor are they subject to the emotional experiences that characterize personalities. You might say that a nonphysical Teacher *is* its soul. Nonphysical Teachers are impersonal sources of wisdom and compassion that are real but not physical. You cannot assess the wisdom and compassion of a nonphysical Teacher any more than you can assess the wisdom and compassion of the Universe, no matter how often or hard you try. You also cannot affect the compassion and wisdom of the Universe any more than you can alter the effects of the sun upon the life forms of our planet.

It is not the job of your nonphysical Teachers to make you compassionate and wise. That is your job. They are always there to assist you. If you decide not to take on the job, it doesn't get done. Why blame others for your choice? When the job of becoming wise and compassionate doesn't get done, you continue to live in pain—the pain that you create, not Hitler, bigots, and terrorists. The world that you live in reflects you, not others. Look inside yourself, and you will see it.

A young man who died, a story goes, entered heaven shaking his fist at God.

"Why didn't you do something about all the suffering in the world I just left?"

"I did," replied God. "I created you."

You can use your time on this precious Earth complaining about what others are doing on it, or consciously determining what you are doing on it. Do you want the world to be more loving? Become more loving yourself. Do you want it to be less violent? Become less violent yourself. Make the changes that you want where you have the most leverage—in yourself. In fact, that is the only place you can make them. You can change yourself, but no one else—not even a nonphysical Teacher—can change you.

Overcoming Life's Problems

WHY IS MY LIFE SO DIFFICULT?

Why do some people find their path in life easier than others who seem to struggle and get nowhere?

No one's life on the Earth is easy. The Earth school is a learning environment. You are on the Earth to learn authentic power—the alignment of your personality with your soul. This requires learning how to create what your soul wants to create. It also requires developing the ability to see wisdom and compassion in every challenge that you encounter. If you already had that ability, your experiences would not be as painful because you would look at the challenges in your life differently.

When you judge an experience as unfair, or tragic, or random, you automatically experience anger, emotional withdrawal, depression, fear, or another of the many painful emotions that accompany the perception of yourself as a victim. When you see each of your challenges as an opportunity to discover and change the parts of yourself that feel like a victim rather than the creator of your own experiences, you automatically respond to the challenges in your life with gratitude, and even joy.

Moreover, when you respond to the challenges in your life with gratitude and appreciation, your responses to them change. Instead of reacting with anger, depression, jealousy, rage, or fear, you begin to respond with compassion and wisdom. You become more detached from your painful experiences, and that allows you to see the circumstances of your life more clearly and to respond to them more intelligently.

You "get nowhere" in your life by continuing to respond to the difficulties in your life in the same ways that you have responded to them in the past. Your experiences begin to change when your responses to your challenges begin to change.

Whether your responses change or not is for you to decide.

WHY DO BAD THINGS HAPPEN TO GOOD PEOPLE?

Why do bad things happen to people who are only trying to live good lives?

The circumstances of your life are neither good nor bad. They are appropriate to the needs of your soul. They may or may not be what your personality desires.

Your life is neither good nor bad. It is the vehicle through which your soul experiences the Earth school in order to heal particular aspects of itself. You experience those aspects as the parts of your personality that are angry, judgmental, frightened, depressed, jealous, vengeful, superior, inferior, and all of the other painful ways of experiencing your life.

When you insist on seeing yourself as a victim who deserves better than you are receiving, you position yourself as a victim. This prevents you from using your life as it was designed to be used—to grow spiritually. Every experience that you encounter is the most appropriate experience that it is possible for you to encounter at the moment that you encounter it. Every response that you choose creates consequences that you will experience. That is how the Earth school works. The Earth school continues without class breaks, holidays, or summer vacations. It has no final examinations and you are never tested. You continually encounter experiences that are exquisitely tailored to the needs of your soul.

HOW CAN I HEAL BAD MEMORIES?

I cannot forget some painful experiences. How can I finally heal them?

Learn from them. Regret serves no useful function in spiritual growth. It makes the tree grow crooked. Your experiences are painful to remember because, as you look back on them, you see how you could have spoken or acted otherwise, or how you wish things would have turned out differently. When you indulge in the pain of regret, you walk past the gift that is being offered to you by the Universe. Instead of squandering your energy trying to change in your imagination or memory what cannot be changed, use that energy to change what can be changed—your life. Relive your painful experiences but not to dive once more into trauma and agony. Relive them to discover what intentions you held at the time, and to examine the words that you spoke, and your actions. Compare what you created then with what you want to create now and use your experiences to help you create differently.

After you explore your painful memories in detail with the intention to learn how to create more wisely in the present, let them go. Their purpose is to instruct you, not torment you. Be grateful that you will no longer create again what you created in the past. Set the intention to be aware of old reactions as they surface, and to respond to the circumstances of your life differently. That gives value to your experiences. Pain is merely pain, but pain for a worthy cause is suffering. What is more worthy than your soul—than creating a life through which the energy of your soul can flow unimpeded into the Earth school? What is more worthy than fulfilling your most noble aspirations?

Once you have learned from your painful memories and you

feel confident in your intention to apply what you have learned from them to your life, release them. Imagine each one of them in a helium balloon and that you are holding the strings. Then imagine cutting the strings with a scissors and watching the balloons rising up and up, getting smaller and smaller, until they disappear.

HOW CAN I HANDLE MY NEGATIVITY?

When I find I am upset, what can I do to stop the negativity in me?

When you become upset—angry, sad, jealous, resentful, or any of the other experiences of fear—stop what you are doing and become aware of what you are feeling. Notice what is happening inside yourself. Observe what you are feeling in your body and where. Remind yourself that the thoughts you are thinking and the emotions you are feeling are coming from a part of your personality that is frightened. Ask yourself if you want a frightened part of your personality to be making your decisions for you. Then ask yourself, "What would I do if I were a wise and compassionate person?"

HOW CAN I HEAL MY COMPETITIVE NATURE?

How can I get over making comparisons of myself, my house, or my children to others, and judging that I am better or worse?

Competition is an expression of fear. Fear that you will not be able to take care of yourself. Fear that you are not lovable. Fear that your life is meaningless. The underlying issue is not one of competitiveness, but of fear. Until you address the parts of your personality that are frightened, you will experience the insecurity that expresses itself in your need to compete with others. From the perspective of your soul, there is nothing to compete for. You are a creative and powerful, compassionate and loving spirit. So are your fellow students in the Earth school.

The Universe provides you with what you need. That may not be what your personality desires. The difference between what your soul needs and what your personality desires is a measure of the pain in your life. In other words, the pain in your life results from the divergence between the desires of your personality and the needs of your soul. Authentic power is the experience of having what you need at each moment.

HOW CAN I LET GO OF THE PAIN OF ENDING A RELATIONSHIP?

How does a person learn to let go of the pain, accept, and move on without your partner, when he or she no longer wants to continue the relationship?

Moving on with your life in this situation is no different from moving on with your life in any situation that is painful to you. The pain comes from experiencing the difference between how you would like the world to be and how the world is.

Your emotional pain is not an unfortunate result of external circumstances. It originates inside of you, not outside of you, and its purpose is to direct your attention to parts of your personality that you need to heal. For example, what behaviors or attitudes of yours might have contributed to the end of your relationship? Is it possible you were dominating, or attempting to please, or controlling in some other way? Were you competitive or judgmental? Look into yourself and see what part you played.

Even if you are certain that you had nothing to do with the ending of the relationship, ask yourself why you are in such pain. For example, what expectations did you have? Were your expectations perhaps a burden for your partner? The point is that you can learn more about yourself from your experiences than you can about other people. And you can change yourself with what you learn about yourself, but you cannot change other people. That is for them to do.

HOW CAN I FORGIVE MYSELF IF I DON'T FEEL WORTHY OF FORGIVENESS?

I do not feel that I deserve forgiveness, but I want to forgive myself.
How can I do that?

Forgiveness is an energy dynamic. Not forgiving is like wearing dark sunglasses that gruesomely distort all that you see, and wanting others to see through the same glasses. When you forgive, you lighten your load. It is like leaving behind a heavy weight. Imagine that you are trying to walk through an airport while carrying a big suitcase in each hand with another strapped over your shoulder and another on your back like a backpack. It is difficult and painful work to go anywhere. Forgiving is putting down all of your baggage and leaving it behind. You travel lightly. Forgiveness has nothing to do with worthiness—yours or others'. You and they are both worthy. That is not the issue. The issue is whether you wish to continue to carry your baggage.

HOW CAN I LEARN TO TRUST?

I am in the middle of a huge transition, but I feel fear and uncertainty. How do I fully trust the process?

The process is the unfolding of your life in a context of spiritual growth. Learning to trust this process is no different from trusting it, any more than you can learn to ride a bicycle without riding it. Your skill at bicycle riding increases with practice, but you cannot learn how to ride before you begin to ride.

In the same way, you cannot learn to trust without beginning to experiment with trusting. Trusting that your life is meaningful, that the Universe is wise and compassionate, and that your experiences happen for a reason requires you to challenge your anger, jealousy, vengefulness, greed, and all the other forms of fear. It renders your judgments as useless as they are painful.

Trusting the process does not mean that you relinquish responsibility for what you experience. It means that you look for meaning in all of your experiences, and make the effort to connect your choices with your experiences. It does not require blind faith or believing any expert or authority. It requires that you experiment with your life and entertain the idea that nothing happens without a reason. That reason has to do with your spiritual growth.

Finding Meaning and Purpose

HOW CAN I BECOME THE PERSON I WANT TO BE?

How do I change my ways and behavior to what I want them to be?

The first step in changing yourself is to entertain the idea that you do not have to be the person that you are. In other words, you can consider the possibility that your ways of looking at circumstances, reacting, and thinking are not the ways that everyone perceives, reacts, and thinks. They are your ways of experiencing in this moment, but all of them are not necessarily the ways that you have to be.

Once you see your own thoughts, values, and judgments from this perspective, you will be able to determine whether you want to stay the way that you are or to change. If you choose to stay the way you are, you will continue to create the same types of consequences that you have created in the past. The difference will be that you will know that you have a choice, and that what you experience is what you are choosing to experience.

If you decide to change, you will have to decide what it is about yourself that you want to change, and how to do that. Your intentions create your experience. When you decide to change, that change has already begun. Try intending to create harmony instead of discord, cooperation instead of competition, sharing instead of hoarding, and contributing to others instead of taking from them. If you feel that you already hold these intentions, yet you continue to encounter discord, competition, hoarding, and exploitation in your life, start a search inside yourself—not in others—for the causes of those painful experiences.

Experiment with your life. That is what you have it for.

HOW DOES A PERSON KNOW WHAT HE WAS PUT ON EARTH TO DO?

What is a person's calling?

Every human has a sacred contract that he or she voluntarily entered into with the Universe. Your responsibility while you are in the Earth school is to give the gifts that you were born to give. That is how you fulfill your sacred contract. In order to be able to give the gifts that you were born to give, you must find in yourself those parts of yourself that keep you from doing that. Those are the parts of yourself that are frightened. In other words, they are the parts of you that are angry, jealous, vengeful, avaricious, sad, feel superior or inferior, need to please others, and so on.

Locating and healing those parts of yourself is the process of creating authentic power. You do that by developing emotional awareness and by making responsible choices. As you create authentic power in your life, you become less frightened—less angry, jealous, greedy, etc. At the same time, you gain more freedom to experiment with your life—because you are not frightened to change it.

When you feel that your life has no purpose and you do not know why you are alive, you are not doing what your soul wants you to do. When you know that you are alive for a reason and that what you are doing is that reason, you are filled with enthusiasm, joy, and gratitude. Everything becomes meaningful and worthy of your creativity. That is the experience of authentic power. Therefore, if what you are doing is not satisfying to you, or exciting, or fulfilling, try something else. The more authentic power you develop, the more freedom you will have to experiment with your life and the more desire you will have to experiment with it.

Creating authentic power and fulfilling your sacred contract happen together. As you become authentically powerful, you are drawn naturally to activities that are more meaningful to you, and those are the activities that your soul wants to do.

HOW DO I FIND MY PURPOSE?

I feel so unfulfilled and lonely inside. How do I find my purpose?

You have a purpose, and you are not alone. You are an immortal soul, and as you begin to look at your life from that perspective you will see your experiences differently.

I do not mean that the one who was born on a certain date and will die on a certain date is immortal. Your personality is not immortal, but your soul is. You are an instrument of your soul. A part of you is immortal. As you begin to look at your life from the point of view of that part, you will begin to see that all of your experiences—even those of despair, of having no reason for living, and of being alone—have a purpose.

It is for you to decide whether you will continue to indulge these painful experiences and for how long. Your experiences of being unfulfilled and lonely are powerful, but you can change them. The first step is to recognize that you have the ability to find the parts of your personality that are creating these experiences and change them. The next step is to challenge each of your painful experiences when they come. They will not disappear the first or second or even the tenth time you challenge them, but the more you challenge them, the more they will lose power over you. Eventually their power over you will disintegrate. Each time you challenge a frightened part of your personality, you invoke the assistance of the Universe, and the Universe responds by bringing those painful experiences more frequently into your consciousness so that you can challenge them. That is how to create authentic power, and part of the experience of authentic power is the experience of meaning and purpose.

284 • SOUL QUESTIONS

WHAT IS THE SINGLE BEST THING I CAN DO FOR MYSELF?

What is the single best thing I can do to grow spiritually?

Realize that you are worthy of your life and live it accordingly.

The Learning Process

HOW CAN EVERYONE IN A COMMUNITY BE EQUAL?

Please explain "equality." How can everyone in a community or organization be equal when some are more responsible than others?

All forms of Life have the same value. All are precious. None is more precious or valuable than another and none is less valuable or precious than another. You and your nonphysical Teachers share this equality, although your nonphysical Teachers know and live in more wisdom and compassion than you. Parents and children are equals, although parents have responsibility for the care and development of children. It would be inappropriate to say that an infant must care for its parents because it is equal with its parents. Yet which is more valuable—the parent or the child? Both are equally valuable. Both are precious.

Some individuals have stronger bodies than others. An inequality exists. Some are more artistic than others and some are more intellectual. These inequalities are temporary inequalities in the flow of evolution. Each soul has been female and male, old and young, strong and weak, quick and slow, and kind and brutal. To insist that an individual with a small body do the physical work of an individual with a large strong body is inappropriate and does not recognize the inequality that exists.

To say that an individual with a small body is unequal to an individual with a large body is inappropriate and does not recognize the equality that exists among souls and among all forms of Life.

The experience of the equality of all forms of Life is reverence. When reverence becomes central to the human experience, the exploitation of all forms of Life by the human species, and the exploitation of humans by humans will cease. That exploitation cannot be stopped by insisting that all humans be considered equally strong-bodied, weak-bodied, artistic, intellectual, or equal in any of the many ways that make each personality unique.

HOW CAN I TELL THE DIFFERENCE BETWEEN WANTS AND NEEDS?

I have problems differentiating between my wants and my authentic needs. How do I do this and still enjoy material things without feeling guilty?

The creation of authentic power requires that you distinguish between your artificial needs and your authentic needs. Your artificial needs are those you experience in order to make yourself known and to influence those around you. You may, for example, feel you need to have quiet when someone is listening to the television, but if you look at that need or one like it, you will see that your real need is to control another person.

Attempting to manipulate and control is the pursuit of external power. This is not the same as the pursuit of authentic power. The Universe provides you with your authentic needs. You have a need to express the love that is within you, the care and affection for Life, the concern for our Earth, and the desire to be in companionship with your fellow humans. The volume of the television, the size of your car or home, the color of your clothes, or the cut of your hair are not authentic needs.

Do not confuse the issue of guilt with the distinction between authentic and artificial needs. Are your intentions to create harmony, cooperation, sharing, and reverence for Life? Are they to support those around you in doing the same? Do you delight in the flowering of compassion and the appearance of wisdom in yourself and others? Is your life at the service of all forms of Life? If so, guilt cannot be a part of your experience. Guilt is an experience of fear. The fundamental fear that all students in the Earth school share is not being worthy of life. In its naked form it appears as the "survivor guilt" felt by so many soldiers and individuals who have survived traumas while others have not. They feel guilty to be whole while their comrades are crippled. They feel guilty to be alive while their comrades are dead. The young boy whose brother drowns suffers guilt because he lives and his brother does not. This fear is real, powerful, and deep. To touch it is to touch the pain of powerlessness, of feeling that you do not deserve to be alive, that you are not loved and are unlovable, that you are intrinsically defective and ugly at your core.

This fear cannot be assuaged by material things. It can only be removed by addressing it directly and healing it with your choices by finding, challenging, and changing the frightened parts of your personality, which are those parts that accumulate things to make themselves feel safe, worthy, and lovable. Satisfying your artificial needs is the pursuit of external power. You fear that you will not obtain what you need and you fear that you will lose what you have. Satisfying your authentic needs serves the intentions of your soul and feeds your soul. You are grateful for what you have and you have what you need. A large house can be the fulfillment of an artificial need—one created by fear—or a temporary tool that you have acquired in your pursuit of authentic power.

The creation of authentic power does not involve justifying your activities or decisions. It requires setting your intention to create harmony, cooperation, sharing, and reverence for Life and experiencing what those intentions create.

HOW DO I KNOW WHEN I AM RUNNING AWAY OR MOVING TO MY NEXT LESSON IN LIFE?

When I think I have learned a lesson, is it okay to move on to the next or am I running away without knowing it?

You cannot run away from the lessons that you need to learn. When you learn them, there is no longer anything to run away from. For example, if your challenge is to live without anger and judgment, the Universe will provide you with continual opportunities to become angry and judge others. These opportunities will not stop coming until you realize the painful experiences your anger and judgment are creating in your life. When that happens, there is no longer a need for you to continue learning in the same way. That is what happens when you complete a lesson in the Earth school—you change. In this case, you stop looking at fellow souls with anger and judgment. That is spiritual growth.

CAN AWARENESS OVERCOME TEMPTATION?

Is awareness the key that allows temptation to lose power? To make that which is unconscious, conscious?

Temptation is the dynamic through which you are able to become aware of parts of your personality that intend to create consequences that would be painful if you acted on them. The temptation has no power over you, but these parts of your personality do and until you acknowledge and change them, they will act as they choose. In other words, temptation brings the intentions of frightened parts of your personality into your awareness and forces you to make a choice—to act on them or not.

If you choose to act on the intentions that temptation presents to you, you choose to actually live through the experiences and create consequences for yourself and others. If you choose not to act on those intentions, you avoid the painful consequences they would have created and instead evolve directly through your choice.

Look at temptation as a dress rehearsal for a negative Karmic event. It is a gift from the Universe that allows you to see negativity in yourself that would create painful consequences if it were to remain unconscious. Your temptations are opportunities that the Universe graciously provides you to see negativity in yourself so that you can heal it before it spills over into the lives of others and creates consequences that you would not want to experience.

DO INTENTION AND MOTIVATION MEAN THE SAME?
Can you interchange the word "motivation" for "intention"?

Yes. Motivation, reason for acting, and intention all mean the same thing. Your intention is a quality of consciousness that you bring to an action. For example, if you donate money to charities because you want to be known as a generous person, or to think of yourself as generous, your intention is to gain, not to give. If your intention is to give, you will not be concerned with how your actions are perceived. If you give because you want tax benefits for yourself, your intention, again, is to gain even though you appear to be giving. Recognizing your intention when you act is important because your intention, not your action, creates the consequences you will experience.

WHAT IS THE DIFFERENCE BETWEEN A HEALTHY BOUNDARY AND EMOTIONAL WITHDRAWAL?

How do I know whether I am setting a healthy boundary or emotionally withdrawing?

The difference is intention. When you set healthy boundaries you do not blame or judge others. When you set boundaries to make a point, win a point, inflict punishment, etc., you do both. Emotional withdrawal is a form of pursuing external power—the ability to manipulate and control. Healthy boundaries are the expression of authentic power. Your intention is to become whole, not to hold others responsible for your experiences.

DOES DOUBT HAVE A PURPOSE?
What is the purpose of doubt in our lives?

There is no purpose for doubt in the most fundamental questions of our lives. Doubt is the absence of trust. It is an indicator that you are experiencing issues of trust and you doubt that the Universe is wise and compassionate. You doubt that your life has meaning, you doubt that you have a reason to be alive. You doubt that your experiences are perfect for your spiritual growth given the wisdom of the choices you have made. Doubt alerts you to place your attention and apply your will to an appropriate part of your personality. Doubt is fear. The fundamental question is how you will learn wisdom—through fear and doubt or through love and trust. No one can make that decision for you. The same is true for everyone. The question of whether you will learn through fear and doubt or love and trust is the one that confronts every individual, every moment of every day.

What do you choose?

HOW CAN I FEEL AUTHENTICALLY EMPOWERED EVERY DAY?

How do I get through every day feeling authentically empowered?

You cannot feel authentically empowered without creating authentic power. To do that you must find and heal the parts of your personality that generate your painful emotions. As you do, you become able to create without interference those parts. Strive to become aware of everything you are feeling all the time. When you feel impatient or frightened or angry or sad, experience what you are feeling in your body, and then choose how you will respond to your circumstances. You do not have to act in anger merely because you are angry, or withdraw emotionally because you are frightened. When you choose to respond instead of react mindlessly—which means robotically and habitually—you challenge a frightened part of your personality.

Authentic power is the experience of meaning and purpose in your life. It is being fully engaged in the present moment. It is creating with an empowered heart without attachment to the outcome. The frightened parts of your personality prevent this experience. You cannot feel as though your life is purposeful, meaningful, and creative when you are sad, frightened, angry, jealous, or vengeful. These frightened parts will not disappear immediately when you choose to create authentic power, but as you challenge them again and again, they will lose their power over you and you will gain power over them.

It requires your choice. That is how to create authentic power.

HOW CAN I REMEMBER MY SPIRIT?

How do I remember my spirit in the midst of a very negative situation?

This question lies at the heart of creating authentic power. You can remember your spirit by remembering that the circumstance you are in is designed for your benefit. Sometimes that is difficult to do, but if you hold the thought that no matter how challenging the circumstance may be, it is designed to help you grow spiritually, that thought will allow you to see the situation differently. Instead of taking your situation so personally, ask yourself what you can learn from it. Instead of accusing and blaming others, even if you feel outraged or treated unjustly, ask what you can learn about yourself.

Once you develop this practice you will find the deep learning that is waiting for you. Eventually you will discover that you are grateful for your experiences, including the most difficult. It is easy to see yourself as a victim, but that leads to more of what you have created in the past. By looking for the wisdom and the compassion that is waiting for you in your most difficult experiences, you will change your life.

DO MY SURROUNDINGS PREVENT ME FROM CREATING AUTHENTIC POWER?

Do I need to isolate myself until I am strong enough to continue in the real world?

Ask yourself if you are tired and need to rest, or if you are running away from your life. Your circumstances are not obstacles to creating authentic power. They are opportunities for you to create authentic power. Creating authentic power requires you to become aware of everything you are feeling. When you isolate yourself from the difficult circumstances in your life, you isolate yourself from opportunities to develop emotional awareness.

Creating authentic power also requires responsible choice—choices that create consequences for which you are willing to assume responsibility. The difficult situations in your life provide you with opportunities to be patient with others instead of becoming angry or judgmental, and to speak from your heart instead of your head. By speaking from your heart I do not mean to speak sentimentally, or attempt to make others feel better, but to speak from the most grounded, healthy, and appropriate place you can attain in the moment. You lose these opportunities when you isolate yourself from others.

The real world is a world of compassion and wisdom. It is a living Universe that supports your spiritual growth in every way. The brutality, suffering, and violence in our world are there because we created them. The remedy is not to withdraw from what we have created, but to create differently.

CAN I REMAIN A CHRISTIAN (OR JEW, HINDU, MUSLIM, BUDDHIST) AND CREATE AUTHENTIC POWER?

I was born again through Jesus Christ, but it would be incredibly exciting for me to think that I can be true to my faith and still explore authentic power. Is that possible?

Authentic power is the alignment of your personality with your soul. Your soul is that part of you that longs for harmony, cooperation, sharing, and reverence for Life. Every religion honors these goals. You will not be less Christian or Hindu, Muslim, Buddhist, or Jewish as you become more effective in achieving those goals.

The exploration of authentic power does not require abandoning your faith. Most Jews, Hindus, Muslims, Buddhists, Christians, and nonreligious people seek lives of meaning, purpose, and fulfillment. They long to live joyfully and to contribute all that they can to Life. These are the experiences of authentic power. You can begin your exploration of authentic power from where you are. You can develop emotional awareness and experiment with the idea of making your choices responsibly—experiment with assuming full responsibility for the consequences that your choices create. That is how you begin to experience for yourself what is appropriate for you and what is not. The more you explore your emotions, choices, and intentions, the clearer will become the value that each has for you. You cannot love someone else enough to sacrifice your life for him or her, as the Christ did, much less give up anything of value to you, until you have thoroughly explored all that you are and can act with the authority of your soul.

That is authentic power.

DO YOU HAVE A MEDITATION PRACTICE?
What do you do to balance and center yourself?

My life is my meditation, and everything I do in it is part of my meditation. Here are some of the things that I do: I observe my emotions in terms of the physical sensations in my body, especially my solar plexus, chest, and throat areas, as often as I can remember. I challenge frightened parts of my personality (anger, jealousy, resentment, vengefulness, feeling superior or inferior, anxiety, fear, etc.) when they are active (I hurt) and I cultivate the loving parts (contentment, gratitude, appreciation, joy, etc.) when they are active (my physical sensations are pleasing). I also pay close attention to my intentions when I speak or act. If I forget, I pay attention to them again when I remember. My intention is my reason, or motivation, for acting. It is also what creates the consequences I will encounter. When my intention is an intention of my soul—harmony, cooperation, sharing, or reverence for Life—I know I am creating authentic power. When it is not, I know that a frightened part of my personality is active and creating painful consequences for me.

I open to what my experiences tell me about myself, rather than what they might tell me about other people. I especially notice what I do not like about other people because I know that my reactions to other people show me parts of my personality that I am not aware of or that I have been avoiding. I strive to find the internal causes of my experiences and to change them rather than looking for the causes of my experiences in other people and trying to change other people.

I set my intentions for the day in the morning, and for the night before I sleep, and whenever I feel the need during the day. I also try to enjoy myself and the perfection of the present moment.

AN INVITATION TO
THE SEAT OF THE SOUL INSTITUTE

I would like to extend to you a warm welcome to join me on an exciting journey to the soul. In this amazing time of spiritual awakening, the door to new dimensions of consciousness is now opening before millions of us, and soon will open for all. What you do with your new consciousness is for you to decide, and no one can decide it for you. When you choose to align your personality with your soul—to create harmony, cooperation, sharing, and reverence for Life—you create authentic power.

Authentic power is the experience of meaning, vitality, creativity, and joy. Humbleness, clarity, forgiveness, and love are the characteristics of an authentically empowered individual. Creating authentic power requires emotional awareness, because your emotions are the force field of your soul; conscious choice of your intentions, because they create your experiences; consulting your intuition, because it can show you options you might not have considered and their consequences; and trust in the Universe. It also requires commitment, courage, compassion, and conscious communications and actions.

My spiritual partner, Linda Francis, and I have created the Seat of the Soul Institute. Its vision is a world in which spiritual growth is the highest priority, and all of its programs and activities are designed to support you in creating authentic power and spiritual partnerships. Please visit us at our website and learn how our activities and programs can support you, and join us in the ever-expanding spiritual partnership community that is occurring naturally as more and more people make spiritual growth—the creation of authentic power—their highest priority.

www.seatofthesoul.com

Also, please feel free to email me at:

gary@seatofthesoul.com

We are all now on the journey to the soul. I hope to see you sometime soon.

Love,
Gary Zukav

INDEX

personality (*cont.*)
  as energy tool, 224
  feeling at odds with, 224
  unconscious parts of, 240–41
perspective, 56–58
Plato, 218
positivity, 35, 166–67, 273
potential, 165, 179, 218
power:
  authentic, *see* authentic power
  authentic empowerment, 295
  creative, 200
  external, 45, 288, 289
  of thoughts, 166–67
powerlessness, 34
prayer, 176
priorities, 115–16
projection, 194
projection recall, 194–95
protection, 191–92
purpose, 283, 295

quality of life, 140–41
quantum logic, 56

Ram Dass, 112–14
rationalization, 230–31
reflection, 246
regret, 271–72
reincarnation, 159–60
rejection, 33–35, 152
relationships, 182–83, 275
release, 75
religion, and authentic power, 298
repression, 258
resentment, 61–62, 186
resistance, 262
response, 165, 196, 269, 270, 295
responsibility:
  assuming, 49–50, 172
  for giving, 281–82
  in making choices, 200, 247,
    261, 263, 281, 297,
    298
  in reincarnation, 159–60
  teaching, 200
  unequal, 286–87
  for yourself, 42, 243, 277

retreats:
  bonding in, 22–23
  "Celebration of Your Soul," 78–79
  confronting fears in, 28–29
  expectations in, 142–43
  spiritual partnership in, 108–9
revenge, 45–46, 85–87, 135
reverence, 109, 172, 208, 286–87
role models, 199, 202
roots, 63–64

sacred contract, 281–82
sacred practices, 176
satisfaction, in small things, 122
scientific method, 177–78
seasons, 6–7, 10–11, 12–13
Seat of the Soul, The (Zukav), 56, 97
Seat of the Soul Institute, 301–2
security, 71
seeds, 13
self-healing, 185
self-protection, 191–92
self-respect, 88–89
self-responsibility, 42, 243, 277
self-worth, 284
sensations, 97–99
sensory system, 161
September 11 attacks, responses to,
    45–46, 85–87, 130–33, 135
sharing, 66–67, 84, 172, 261
snake skin, 28
snowbound, 66–67, 88–89
soul:
  alignment of personality with, 36, 80,
    96, 158, 172, 196, 216, 228, 268,
    274, 281, 297, 298
  communication after death, 225
  communication with, 109
  departure of, 222
  difference between personality and,
    222–23
  emotions as field force of, 261
  experience of, 220
  goals of, 172
  great, 228–29
  immortality of, 64, 220, 222, 283
  imperfection in, 218–19
  intentions of, 289

ABOUT THE AUTHOR

GARY ZUKAV has for years conveyed the most complex insights in language all can understand. Over and over, he challenges us to see the depth of our potential in the world . . . and to act on that awareness. He is the author of four consecutive *New York Times* bestsellers. In 1979, *The Dancing Wu Li Masters: An Overview of the New Physics* plumbed the depths of quantum physics and relativity, winning The American Book Award for Science. In 1989, *The Seat of the Soul* led the way to seeing the alignment of the personality with the soul as the fulfillment of life and captured the imagination of millions, becoming the #1 *New York Times* bestseller over thirty times and residing on the *New York Times* bestseller list for three years. *Soul Stories* (2000), as well as *The Heart of the Soul: Emotional Awareness* (2001) and *The Mind of the Soul: Responsible Choice* (2003), both co-authored with Linda Francis, also became *New York Times* bestsellers. Six million copies of his books are in print, and translations have been published in twenty-four languages.

Gary Zukav is a co-founder of the Seat of the Soul Institute, a graduate of Harvard with a degree in International Relations, a former U.S. Army Special Forces (Green Beret) officer with Vietnam service, and a grandfather. His gentle presence, humor, and wisdom have endeared him to millions through his appearances on *The Oprah Winfrey Show.* He lives in Oregon with his spiritual partner, Linda Francis, also a co-founder of the Seat of the Soul Institute.

For more information about Gary Zukav, please visit

www.seatofthesoul.com.

Or, to contact Gary, send an email to

gary@seatofthesoul.com.